LIVE THE WORD
COMMENTARY
HEBREWS

DR. JOHN W. STANKO

Live the Word Commentary: Hebrews
by John W. Stanko
Copyright © 2019 John W. Stanko

ISBN # 978-1-63360-115-4

All rights reserved under International Copyright Law. Written permission must be secured from the publisher/author to reproduce, copy, or transmit any part of this book.

Unless otherwise noted, all scripture quotations taken from the Holy Bible, New International Version®, NIV®. Copyright © 1973, 1978, 1984, 2011 by Biblica, Inc.™ Used by permission of Zondervan. All rights reserved worldwide. www.zondervan.com The "NIV" and "New International Version" are trademarks registered in the United States Patent and Trademark Office by Biblica, Inc.

Scripture quotations marked (NKJV) are taken from the NEW KING JAMES VERSION®. Copyright© 1982 by Thomas Nelson, Inc. Used by permission. All rights reserved.

Scripture quotations marked (NAS) are taken from the NEW AMERICAN STANDARD BIBLE®, Copyright© 1960, 1962, 1963, 1968, 1971, 1972, 1973, 1975, 1977, 1995 by The Lockman Foundation. Used by permission.

For Worldwide Distribution Printed in the U.S.A.

Urban Press
P. O. Box 8881
Pittsburgh, PA 15221-0881 USA
412.646.2780

www.urbanpress.us

Introduction

The letter to the Hebrews is not written to a people in one location like a city or a region. It is not written to an individual like Timothy or Titus. The letter is written to a category of people and those were Jews who had put their faith in Christ—or who were perhaps considering doing so—but were wavering in their ongoing commitment. They were not in one area, but were scattered, so this letter had to be passed on from reader to reader for it to reach its target audience.

We don't know who wrote the letter, although there are many theories, but we know one thing: Whoever wrote it loved the believing Jews but was concerned lest they go backwards in their faith walk by returning to Judaism. Thus, the entire letter is an appeal (and an apologetic of sorts) that there can be no way to God the Father except through Christ. Anyone who denies that and turns to another system has no place to go:

> It is impossible for those who have once been enlightened, who have tasted the heavenly gift, who have shared in the Holy Spirit, who have tasted the goodness of the word of God and the powers of the coming age and who have fallen away, to be brought back to repentance. To their loss they are crucifying the Son of God all over again and subjecting him to public disgrace (Hebrews 6:4-6).

This deals a serious blow to those who believed as part of this modern culture of tolerance, that there are many ways to God, that sincerity is the only requirement. If one sincerely believes, then it has to be "right," no matter how wrong it may be. It also deflates the romantic notion that somehow Judaism is on a parallel course with Christianity and that God is working in a dual system because the Jewish people are still His people. That notion seems to have no basis for belief in this letter. Jesus was, is, and will be the only way to God for Jews.

The writer (or writers, for it could have been a collaborative effort) on several occasions pointed out that faith in Christ introduces the believer to better things than were in the Law:

- a better hope (7:19)
- a better covenant (7:22)
- better promises (8:6)
- better sacrifices (9:23)
- better possessions (10:24)
- a better word (Hebrews 12:24).

The implication is clear: Why would anyone who has something that is better return to something else that they know is inferior? That does not make sense, especially in a context where Christ is superior to Moses, and the life of the Spirit better than trying to fulfill the Law. Faith is not a matter of personal preference; it is a matter of God's truth, and God's truth is embodied in Christ and His church.

I mentioned that this letter could have been written by a team, and I lean toward that theory—but I have no proof, only some opinions based on circumstantial evidence. My theory is that Paul was one of the writers who collaborated on this letter. Let me explain why I make that claim.

Paul loved his people, the Jews. He went to the synagogue first no matter where he went, trying to reach them with the message of the gospel, hoping they would accept his testimony of Christ because of his history:

> "When I returned to Jerusalem and was praying at the temple, I fell into a trance and saw the Lord speaking to me. 'Quick!' he said. 'Leave Jerusalem

immediately, because the people here will not accept your testimony about me.' "'Lord,' I replied, 'these people know that I went from one synagogue to another to imprison and beat those who believe in you. And when the blood of your martyr Stephen was shed, I stood there giving my approval and guarding the clothes of those who were killing him.' "Then the Lord said to me, 'Go; I will send you far away to the Gentiles'" (Acts 22:17-21).

Paul argued with the Lord, disagreeing that he was under any danger from the Jews. The Lord knew best, however, and sent him away because his success was not to be among the Jews but rather the Gentiles. What's more, when Paul preached his message of salvation by faith, many believing Jews opposed him, maintaining that the Gentiles who came to Christ by faith still had to keep the Law. Paul wrote Galatians, Romans, and Corinthians to refute their claims in no uncertain terms. This did not win him many friends among the Jews, believing or otherwise. This was confirmed by the apostles when he arrived in Jerusalem later in his ministry:

> When they heard this [God's work among the Gentiles], they praised God. Then they said to Paul: "You see, brother, how many thousands of Jews have believed, and all of them are zealous for the law. They have been informed that you teach all the Jews who live among the Gentiles to turn away from Moses, telling them not to circumcise their children or live according to our customs. What shall we do? They will certainly hear that you have come, so do what we tell you. There are four men with us who have made a vow. Take these men, join in their purification rites and

pay their expenses, so that they can have their heads shaved. Then everyone will know there is no truth in these reports about you, but that you yourself are living in obedience to the law. As for the Gentile believers, we have written to them our decision that they should abstain from food sacrificed to idols, from blood, from the meat of strangled animals and from sexual immorality" (Acts 21:20-25).

If Paul would have identified himself to believing Jews who were wavering in their faith, they would not have received what he had to say. Therefore, Paul had input into the letter (remember, this is my theory) but someone else wrote it, otherwise people would have recognized Paul's style and maybe even his handwriting.

At the end of the day, God didn't want us to know who wrote it and I am fine with that. What's more important is the message, and this message was an urgent SOS to believing Jews not to go "back" but to keep pressing on in Christ. We can only hope that many who were considering a retreat to Judaism and the Law changed their minds once they read this appeal.

This letter was probably circulated right before the fall of Jerusalem in 70 AD, so things in the Roman Empire were tense for the Jews and their nation. God was about to fulfill promises Jesus made concerning the destruction of the Temple, and many believing Jews were probably disillusioned at what had become of their idealistic expectations of what God was going to do to restore the throne of David. As they reconsidered their faith, Hebrews made a brilliant defense of the superiority of Christ in all things spiritual. He was and is above angels, Moses, the Law, and the sacrificial system that had become the backbone of Jewish life. Those wavering Jews had a decision to make, but the writer of Hebrews saw only one logical choice: faithfulness to the gospel of Christ. That is a good message and reminder for us today.

Living the Word

The *Live the Word Commentaries* all have the same format. I have broken down the letter to the Hebrews by chapters and then by passages. After each passage, I comment on individual verses, occasionally grouping two or more verses together that made the comments more cohesive. As you read, I have included questions to help you apply the content in bold so they literally jump out at you. Perhaps as you skim the pages, a question may attract your interest and that will spark you to do some more reading about that verse or passage.

In a few places, I have inserted prayers in italics that you can pray. I have liberally sprinkled cross references to other parts of Scripture throughout the commentary, so you can have a short Bible or devotional study if you so choose. My objective is to help you *apply* and *live* the Word, so I have included as much of the Word as I saw fit to help you understand and then live out the verses in Hebrews.

There you have a quick overview of my commentaries and this volume on the letter to the Hebrews. I pray that God will open your eyes to see as the psalmist prayed in Psalm 119:18: "Open my eyes that I may see wonderful things in your law." May you see wonderful things, but then may you be blessed according to Jesus' words in John 13:17: "Now that you know these things, you will be blessed *if you do them*" (emphasis added).

John W. Stanko, D. Min.
Pittsburgh, PA
June 2019

1

In the past God spoke to our forefathers through the prophets at many times and in various ways, ²but in these last days he has spoken to us by his Son, whom he appointed heir of all things, and through whom he made the universe. ³The Son is the radiance of God's glory and the exact representation of his being, sustaining all things by his powerful word. After he had provided purification for sins, he sat down at the right hand of the Majesty in heaven. ⁴So he became as much superior to the angels as the name he has inherited is superior to theirs.

1:1-2 The main message to the Hebrew reader was that the revelation of Christ was God's most authoritative, complete, and final message. This letter was written to Jews who were not new to the faith, but who were obviously discouraged and questioning their decision to put their faith in Christ. The writer was urging them *not* to return to their former way of life, but to see Jesus as a prophetic revelation from God that was consistent with and superior to past revelations from God.

Jesus was and is the message from God. Everything is from Him and about Him. John wrote, "Through him all things were made; without him nothing was made that has been made" (John 1:3). John continued, "The Word became flesh and made his dwelling among us. We have seen his glory, the glory of the One and Only, who came from the Father, full of grace and truth" (John 1:14).

Jesus is the Word, and a word is the basic component of communication. Therefore, God the Father has spoken through His Son, the Word. The writer was urging the Hebrews not to consider another Word, for Jesus was it. Period. **Can you see the relevance of this message for today's world? Can you see how unpopular this is based on the prevailing mindset that whatever one believes is correct?**

1:3-4 Since Jesus is in heaven at the right hand of the Father, He is superior to the angels. No vision or revelation about angels can ever surpass the greatness of His majesty. No angel can radiate the glory of God like Jesus could and does. Jesus is the exact representation of the Father. I will not go into the Greek words used here, but it is clear that Jesus is of the same essence with the Father but a unique person all the same:

> He is the image of the invisible God, the firstborn over all creation. For by him all things were created: things in heaven and on earth, visible and invisible, whether thrones or powers or rulers or authorities; all things were created by him and for him. He is before all things, and in him all things hold together (Colossians 1:15-18).
>
> For in Christ all the fullness of the Deity lives

in bodily form, and you have been given fullness in Christ, who is the head over every power and authority (Colossians 2:9-11).

Jesus had a specific purpose in coming to earth and that was to provide purification for sins as the sacrificial Lamb of God. Once He accomplished that, He sat down at the right hand of God, symbolic of His great power and the honor ascribed to Him. It is symbolic because God does not have a right hand, but the image is for us to grasp the position, authority, and rank of Jesus.

Is Jesus the focal point of your worship and attention? He should and must be. Don't let *any* doctrine, movement, fad, vision, denomination, or teaching take the place only Jesus should have in your life. There can be no question that the writer saw Jesus as preeminent over all beings and things, deserving of the highest praise and honor. The implication to a Jewish believer would have been clear, presenting the question, **How can you consider going back to Judaism in light of this tremendous revelation of Christ? How can you consider sharing your loyalties with any other movement, philosophy, or religion?** Jesus is Lord and is worthy of all honor and glory.

> [5]For to which of the angels did God ever say, "You are my Son; today I have become your Father"? Or again, "I will be his Father, and he will be my Son"? [6]And again, when God brings his firstborn into the world, he says, "Let all God's angels worship him." [7]In speaking of the angels he says, "He makes his angels winds, his servants flames of fire." [8]But about the Son he says, "Your throne, O God, will last for

ever and ever, and righteousness will be the scepter of your kingdom.

1:5 Here the writer of Hebrews quoted Psalm 2:7, which Paul quoted during his sermon as seen in Acts 13:

"We tell you the good news: What God promised our fathers he has fulfilled for us, their children, by raising up Jesus. As it is written in the second Psalm: 'You are my Son; today I have become your Father'" (Acts 13:32-33).

This raises an interesting point. Some referred to Jesus as the Son of God in His earthly ministry. It seems that Paul in his Acts 13 sermon considered this Sonship to have been confirmed or revealed not at Jesus' birth, but at His resurrection. While Jesus' birth took place in obscurity, His resurrection took place publicly, with many people seeing Jesus during His crucifixion and after His resurrection. It is His death and resurrection, not His birth, which established that Jesus was God's Son.

1:6 While it seems the writer was referring to Jesus' birth at this point, it appears to be a bit of a bad translation. Without getting technical, this verse also seems to point to Jesus' resurrection, where the Father brought Him back into the "living world" after death. It would make more sense for this to be true, given the preceding verses.

It is not quite clear what Old Testament verse the writer was referring to in this case, perhaps Psalm 97:7: "All who worship images are put to shame, those who boast in idols—worship him, all you gods!"

On occasion, you will find a verse in the New Testament that doesn't quite match the verse as it is found in the Old Testament. That is probably because the New Testament writer was quoting from what is called the Septuagint—the ancient Greek translation of the Hebrew

Old Testament. The Greek Septuagint is a translation "once removed" from the original Hebrew and that does affect the interpretation. But don't worry, the basic meaning is the same and just highlights the problems translators have always faced: How to translate exactly from one language to another when some words and concepts don't exist in the "receptor" language. The most important point to remember here is that the writer simply continued establishing Jesus as superior to any angel.

1:7 The writer quoted Psalm 104:4 in this verse, showing that the angels were simply God's messengers. They could not be equated to or elevated to be superior to Christ, for they were simply serving God and the Son. Don't ever exalt angels to anything beyond what they were and are: God's messengers. They are not to be worshiped, prayed to, or exalted.

1:8 Here the writer referred to Psalm 45:6, which was a verse interpreted as a Messianic reference by the Jews. Whoever wrote this letter had a familiarity with the Old Testament and Jewish religious customs and culture. We cannot fully appreciate how the writer was appealing to and touching the Jewish mind and heart with these last few verses. This was certainly a Hebrew writing and reaching out to Hebrews, someone who loved his people and was concerned that they were about to wander from the true faith in order to return to their Jewish heritage.

As I refer to the "writer" of Hebrews, there are two other options to weigh when considering who authored this letter. Some believe it is the transcription of a sermon, and others believe it was written by a committee or a team of Hebrews who were trying to keep their fellow Jews in the Christian fold. Keep that in mind every time you see the word writer or author.

> ⁹You have loved righteousness and hated wickedness; therefore God, your God, has set you above your companions by anointing you with the oil of joy." ¹⁰He also says, "In the beginning, O Lord, you laid the foundations of the earth, and the heavens are the work of your hands. ¹¹They will perish, but you remain; they will all wear out like a garment. ¹²You will roll them up like a robe; like a garment they will be changed. But you remain the same, and your years will never end." ¹³To which of the angels did God ever say, "Sit at my right hand until I make your enemies a footstool for your feet"? ¹⁴Are not all angels ministering spirits sent to serve those who will inherit salvation?

1:9 This verse is from Psalm 45:7 and makes a fascinating statement that the Messiah would be anointed with the "oil of joy." This indicates that when you are anointed with God's anointing it is a joyful thing—joy is how the anointing is identified and the result it produces in the one with the anointing. In other words, the anointing actually produces or manufactures joy. You will know you are anointed when you have or experience joy as you carry out some activity.

Christ is the Greek word for "anointed one" and Messiah is the Hebrew equivalent. So when you say Jesus Christ, you are saying "Jesus the Anointed One." The anointing was an indication that Jesus was chosen of God, for God set His seal of approval on Jesus by gracing Him to do things not possible apart from God's presence in His life:

You know what has happened throughout Judea, beginning in Galilee after the baptism that John preached—how God anointed Jesus of Nazareth with the Holy Spirit and power, and how he went around doing good and healing all who were under the power of the devil, because God was with him (Acts 10:37-38).

What do you do that when you do it, you have joy? Is that an indication of what you are anointed to do? In all probability, it is. Don't just think in terms of ministry, but in any of life's activities. For example, this means there are anointed artists—people whom God empowers to make art. You must expand your understanding of the anointing to go beyond ministry in church or in things traditionally thought to be "spiritual." **What are you anointed to do, as indicated by your source and release of joy when you do them?**

I realize this is not the standard explanation and application for anointing, which is usually restricted to spiritual activities carried out in a church setting. I have expanded its application outside of church for two reasons, both biblical examples.

The first is found in Isaiah where the prophet was describing a secular king named Cyrus: "This is what the Lord says to *his anointed*, to Cyrus, whose right hand I take hold of to subdue nations before him and to strip kings of their armor, to open doors before him so that gates will not be shut" (Isaiah 45:1, emphasis added). God chose and anointed Cyrus to carry out His will in the nations. The second is found in Exodus 31:

Then the Lord said to Moses, "See, I have chosen Bezalel son of Uri, the son of Hur, of the tribe of Judah, and *I have filled him with the Spirit of God*, with wisdom, with understanding, with knowledge and with all kinds of skills—to make artistic designs for work in gold, silver and bronze, to cut and set stones, to work in wood, and to engage in all kinds of crafts (Exodus 31:1-5, emphasis added).

God filled Bezalel not to preach or prophecy, but to work with his hands to create art. If Bezalel was filled with the Spirit, that indicates he was anointed with the Spirit's presence. Based on these two examples, I ask you once again: **What are you anointed to do?** The key indicator will be the joy you have when you do it.

1:10-12 The writer continued to liberally refer to the Old Testament, this time to Psalm 102:25-27. The author believed God was responsible for creation as reported in Genesis, and also equated Jesus with God. He further believed that creation would "wind down" and come to an end, but God Himself would remain the same. The writer did not believe creation was God, but an expression of God's handiwork. Peter expressed this same view of creation's destiny when he wrote,

> But the day of the Lord will come like a thief. The heavens will disappear with a roar; the elements will be destroyed by fire, and the earth and everything in it will be laid bare. Since everything will be destroyed in this way, what kind of people ought you to be? You ought to live holy and godly lives as you look forward to the day of God and speed its coming. That day will bring about the destruction of the heavens by fire, and the elements will melt in the heat. But in keeping with his promise we are looking forward to a new heaven and a new earth, the home of righteousness (2 Peter 3:10-13).

None of the events of creation's end should cause us concern or fear, for the same God who created everything will create a new heaven and a new earth from what He has already done. We have nothing to fear concerning the end times. Those who write books and make lots of money exploiting the uncertainty and fear of the unknown end times are simply fiction writers who have an incorrect theological context for what they write.

Are you fearful of, even infatuated, with the end of the age? If so, you can relax. The Father has everything under His control. The same God who was the mastermind of creation, which He declared to be good, is the one in control of the transition from this creation we know to the one we have yet to see. He declares that transition and new heaven and earth to be good as well.

1:13-14 Obviously, some Jews venerated angels. The writer was trying to establish that if they venerated angels, they should all the more worship God's Son, for He is above the angels in power, authority, and splendor. The principle is simple: Don't put the things of God above God. Don't be more excited about what God uses to accomplish His will than His will itself.

For example, there are some so excited about faith that they talk about faith instead of the God of their faith. There are others who have seen the reality of demons, healing, and miracles and made them their focus instead of studying the God of those things. **Have you fallen into this tendency?** Keep God supreme in your heart, mind, and attention. Don't be sidetracked by secondary things; make God the primary focus of your life, energy, and devotion.

2

We must pay more careful attention, therefore, to what we have heard, so that we do not drift away. ²For if the message spoken by angels was binding, and every violation and disobedience received its just punishment, ³how shall we escape if we ignore such a great salvation? This salvation, which was first announced by the Lord, was confirmed to us by those who heard him. ⁴God also testified to it by signs, wonders and various miracles, and gifts of the Holy Spirit distributed according to his will.

2:1 This verse gives good advice even by today's standards and needs. We must pay more careful attention to what we have heard. Remember, this letter was addressed to believing Jews. Some in this reading audience could have been present on the day of Pentecost, but by the time of this letter, they were reconsidering whether what they had heard was worth holding on to. They were reconsidering because of God's work among the Gentiles and the de-emphasis of the Law and Jewish customs with which they had been raised and were familiar.

It is easy to "drift away" from the exuberance of your initial faith as life presents challenges and unexpected dilemmas. Perhaps this is what John referred to in Revelation:

> "Yet I hold this against you: You have forsaken your first love. Remember the height from which you have fallen! Repent and do the things you did at first. If you do not repent, I will come to you and remove your lampstand from its place" (Revelation 2:4-5).

Have you forsaken your first love? Drifted away from the zeal and practices of when you first came to faith in Christ? If so, what are prepared to do to reestablish your faith and zeal? The first step would be to repent and then to seek the Lord for a fervent heart on fire for Him and His purpose for you and the world around you.

2:2-3 Some believe the Law was delivered to men through the mediation of angels. This being true, the Old Testament Law thus delivered was binding on the Jews. Now God's son has delivered a greater, more important message and it was confirmed with signs and wonders. This message could not be treated casually or abandoned for a message of lesser importance. The Law delivered by the Son would be greater than the Law of angels, which was difficult for the Jews to accept. They first had to accept that Jesus was indeed the Son who delivered this message of a new Law, the Law of grace in the Son.

2:4 Jesus' ministry was full of "signs and wonders," but so were the ministries of Peter, John, and Paul. God always provides proof for those who are interested in receiving it. Those whose hearts are hardened will reject these proofs since they are entrenched in their own way of thinking and acting, as we saw in these accounts:

> Even after Jesus had done all these miraculous signs in their presence, they still would not believe in him. This was to fulfill the word of Isaiah the prophet: "Lord, who has believed our message and to whom has the arm of the Lord been revealed?" (John 12:37-38)

> The apostles performed many miraculous signs and wonders among the people. And all the believers used to meet together in Solomon's Colonnade (Acts 5:12-13).

> I will not venture to speak of anything except what Christ has accomplished through me in leading the Gentiles to obey God by what I have said and done—by the power of signs and miracles, through the power of the Spirit. So from Jerusalem all the way around to Illyricum, I have fully proclaimed the gospel of Christ (Romans 15:18-20).

It would make sense to me that, if this is how God presented the gospel then, He will do it the same way today. These miracles were not an accommodation to the mentality of the people, but a confirmation of God's great love and the importance of the gospel message. We should expect and even look for miracles today as confirmation of God's work among the nations to establish the gospel of the Son as the supreme act of God's grace and mercy.

> [5]It is not to angels that he has subjected the world to come, about which we are speaking. [6]But there is a place where someone has testified: "What is man that you are mindful of him, the son of

> man that you care for him? ⁷You made him a little lower than the angels; you crowned him with glory and honor ⁸and put everything under his feet." In putting everything under him, God left nothing that is not subject to him. Yet at present we do not see everything subject to him.

2:5 The term in this verse of the "world to come" appears to refer to this present age in which Christ has been exalted to the right hand of the Father. Even if the writer was referring to the next age, the point remains the same: Christ is superior to any angel, especially the angels who administered the Law.

2:6-8 It seems like the writer didn't quite know where the verse was in the Old Testament to which he was referring when he wrote, "Someone has testified." This seems to be a Middle Eastern method of honor and respect when quoting someone great. Here the writer quoted David and Psalm 8:4-6 verbatim from the Septuagint, the Greek translation of the Hebrew Old Testament. Therefore, the writer definitely knew what he was quoting and probably had it in front of him while he was writing.

What's more, some believe Hebrews was the transcript of a preached message given to Jews all over the world by the author, as mentioned earlier. The preacher would not have had a Bible to use like we have today, so he could have quoted the verse without knowing the specific location of the verse. The chapters and verses were not added until centuries later, so it would have been more difficult to locate or identify a verse when Hebrews was composed.

God has great love for Adam's race of fallen, sinful beings. He has exalted mankind to the head of His creation and has worked through Christ to subject all things to man's dominion, as was originally intended with Adam and Eve in the Garden. Their sin marred God's work, but Christ came to restore all things to the Father's original plan.

Let's be more specific about what was established and lost in the Garden of Eden. The Lord introduced five rules or life for mankind in the first two chapters of Genesis. They were:

1. Fellowship with God – Genesis 2:15-17
2. Purposeful work – see Genesis 1:28
3. Expressed creativity – see Genesis 2:18-20
4. Teamwork – see Genesis 2:20b-23
5. Rest – see Genesis 2:2-3

When Adam and Eve sinned, those five practices did not go away, but were tainted and affected negatively. They were still God's plan for His human creation, but man expressed or ignored them because the first parents ate of tree of knowledge of God and evil. Instead of God directing those life expressions, people took them over and expressed them as they saw fit. They rested or not, worked with those they chose to work with, increasingly used their creativity to create idols, selected a purpose they wanted, and ignored God's directives, thus insisting on fellowship with Him based on their own terms.

When Jesus came, He came not just to restore fellowship with God, He came to reconcile *all* things, and those things include the other four expressions of human experience: purpose, creativity, teamwork, and rest:

> The Son is the image of the invisible God, the firstborn over all creation. For in him all things were created: things in heaven and on earth, visible and invisible, whether thrones or powers or rulers or authorities; all things have been created

through him and for him. He is before all things, and in him all things hold together. And he is the head of the body, the church; he is the beginning and the firstborn from among the dead, so that in everything he might have the supremacy. For God was pleased to have all his fullness dwell in him, *and through him to reconcile to himself all things, whether things on earth or things in heaven, by making peace through his blood, shed on the cross* (Colossians 1:15-20, emphasis added).

The Church has historically emphasized one of those five objectives for mankind, and that is fellowship with God. Jesus came not only to restore fellowship but also to reconcile people to God's design for them, which includes purpose, creativity, effective teamwork, and spiritual rest.

Getting back to Hebrews, the subject of this passage seems to point to Christ and not to mankind in general. For a time, Christ was a little lower than the angels, for He was subject to death as we all are (angels are not mortal and cannot die, so mankind is a little lower than they are). All things were placed under Christ, although we see most of humanity and its institutions rebelling against Christ's rule—for now:

Your attitude should be the same as that of Christ Jesus: Who, being in very nature God, did not consider equality with God something to be grasped, but made himself nothing, taking the very nature of a servant, being made in human likeness. And being found in appearance as a man, he humbled himself and became obedient to death—even death on a cross! Therefore God exalted him to the highest place and gave him the name that is above every name, that at the name of Jesus every knee should bow, in heaven and on earth and under the earth, and every tongue confess that Jesus Christ is Lord, to the glory of God the Father (Philippians 2:5-11).

I pray also that the eyes of your heart may be enlightened in order that you may know the hope to which he has called you, the riches of his glorious inheritance in the saints, and his incomparably great power for us who believe. That power is like the working of his mighty strength, which he exerted in Christ when he raised him from the dead and seated him at his right hand in the heavenly realms, far above all rule and authority, power and dominion, and every title that can be given, not only in the present age but also in the one to come. And God placed all things under his feet and appointed him to be head over everything for the church, which is his body, the fullness of him who fills everything in every way (Ephesians 1:17-23).

I once cut off the head of a snake in my neighbor's yard. While that snake was decapitated, it writhed and twisted for a long time after the fact and tried to slither away without a head. That is how it is with creation. It has been subjected to Christ, but it continues to twist and turn in agony, as if it still has a life of its own. In the fullness of time, it will stop its writhing and take its place under the feet of Christ and His followers.

> ⁹But we see Jesus, who was made a little lower than the angels, now crowned with glory and honor because he suffered death, so that by the grace of God he might taste

death for everyone. ¹⁰In bringing many sons to glory, it was fitting that God, for whom and through whom everything exists, should make the author of their salvation perfect through suffering. ¹¹Both the one who makes men holy and those who are made holy are of the same family. So Jesus is not ashamed to call them brothers. ¹²He says, "I will declare your name to my brothers; in the presence of the congregation I will sing your praises."

2:9 What a simple but profound statement the writer made in this verse. We see Jesus because He came from heaven in human flesh, a man like us in every way except sin. He is now sitting at the right hand of the Father, in honor and glory, having been raised from the dead. Jesus died for everyone, so that all could have access to God by faith. This was an act of God's grace to a fallen race in need of a Redeemer and Savior.

This one sentence summarized the Christian faith, which was then presented to a group of believing Jews who were considering a return to Judaism. The truth could not have been presented in a clearer, more concise way. Since the first century, however, Jews have rejected this truth en masse, stumbling over the suffering Savior who died on a cross as Jesus did:

> Where is the wise person? Where is the teacher of the law? Where is the philosopher of this age? Has not God made foolish the wisdom of the world? For since in the wisdom of God the world through its wisdom did not know him, God was pleased through the foolishness of what was preached to save those who believe. Jews demand

signs and Greeks look for wisdom, but we preach Christ crucified: a stumbling block to Jews and foolishness to Gentiles, but to those whom God has called, both Jews and Greeks, Christ the power of God and the wisdom of God. For the foolishness of God is wiser than human wisdom, and the weakness of God is stronger than human strength (1 Corinthians 1:20-25).

2:10 Jesus was not imperfect in any way. Yet His death made Him "complete," in the sense that He had to die to open the way to God for us. Jesus' suffering also enabled Him to experience firsthand the plight of His fallen creatures. Jesus' human experience made Him the "complete" Savior, not just decreeing salvation for His subjects, but earning it for them through His death, while identifying completely with their human condition.

I am always cautious when describing issues such as are raised in this verse. I don't want to take away from Jesus' magnificence, perfection, or divinity in any way. Personally, I find that words sometimes escape me when I try to explain the wonder of God's plan in Christ. I know it must be explained, but I don't feel I am the best one to do that.

2:11 Jesus isn't just our Savior and Redeemer; He is also our elder Brother. That means we are part of the same family. Jesus partook of our flesh so He could become a sacrifice to God for us. Since "my flesh" and "my race" were the problem, Jesus took on that flesh and became part of that race to be a sacrifice *from* our race to *save* our race. Now He has made us holy through His sacrifice.

Jesus can identify with whatever problem we are encountering because He has felt what we feel. He felt rejection on the cross; He was even tempted to take a numbing drug while on the cross (which He refused). Yes, Jesus knows pain, sorrow, temptation, and grief—just like we do—and He knows it because He has been where we are.

That is why we can pray to Him, not as a distant God, but as a brother who knows and is ready to help. **Do you see Jesus as an ever-present help in time of trouble, or is He too distant to be of much help to you? If He seems far away, why do you think that is? What can you do to correct it?**

2:12 Here the writer quoted Psalm 22:2. It was God's plan all along for Jesus to become like "His brothers" so that under one God and Father, a family of believers could declare God's matchless praise. **Why would anyone want to abandon this family, unless religious tradition had so misinterpreted who and what the Messiah would be that they, in disillusionment, considered a return to the dead but predictable and culturally-acceptable Jewish traditions?**

The writer made the choices clear. The believing Jews could choose a living Messiah who created a family under God's Fatherhood, or a dead religion that bound people together in lifeless form and tradition. In some ways, the choice is the same today even for those who consider themselves part of the Christian tradition. **Do you want to be part of a family or part of a religious system? Do you want a living relationship or an institution full of tradition but void of life?**

> [13]And again, "I will put my trust in him." And again he says, "Here am I, and the children God has given me." [14]Since the children have flesh and blood, he too shared in their humanity so that by his death he might destroy him who holds the power of death-that is, the devil—[15]and

free those who all their lives were held in slavery by their fear of death. ¹⁶For surely it is not angels he helps, but Abraham's descendants. ¹⁷For this reason he had to be made like his brothers in every way, in order that he might become a merciful and faithful high priest in service to God, and that he might make atonement for the sins of the people. ¹⁸Because he himself suffered when he was tempted, he is able to help those who are being tempted.

2:13 Whoever wrote this letter (and it is my opinion that the Apostle Paul at least collaborated with someone in writing it) certainly knew the Old Testament. They ran off a series of verses, all of which were considered Messianic verses by the Jews—passages that spoke of the Messiah to come. The writer was making his case that Jesus was the promised Messiah, reminding these believing Hebrew readers that they had chosen to believe in God's Anointed One. In this verse, the writer referenced Psalm 18:2 and Isaiah 8:18.

There is much value in knowing Scripture. I urge you to learn, study, enroll in Bible classes, and do all you can to know the Word.

2:14-18 Who could ever conceive of God taking on the form of His creation, suffering, and then dying so His creation could be set free? What a magnificent plan. What we could not do for ourselves, God did for us. As mentioned earlier, Jesus became like us in every way except sin. I heard a preacher say once that our flesh sits at the right hand of God. Jesus sits in heaven and intercedes for us and represents us well, because He is one of us.

Because Jesus is a man, He understands temptation, and that enables us to go to Him for help when we are tempted. I am always surprised by how many people run from God when they are tempted and even when they sin. I try to make it my practice to run *to* Him in those times, not from Him. **In what direction are you running right now? Toward Him or away from Him?** I urge you to make Jesus your Refuge, your Strong Tower, your Strength, and your Source of help in every and any situation.

3

Therefore, holy brothers, who share in the heavenly calling, fix your thoughts on Jesus, the apostle and high priest whom we confess. ²He was faithful to the one who appointed him, just as Moses was faithful in all God's house. ³Jesus has been found worthy of greater honor than Moses, just as the builder of a house has greater honor than the house itself. ⁴For every house is built by someone, but God is the builder of everything. ⁵Moses was faithful as a servant in all God's house, testifying to what would be said in the future. ⁶But Christ is faithful as a son over God's house. And we are his house, if we hold on to our courage and the hope of which we boast.

3:1 How simple yet profound this command is: Fix your thoughts on Jesus. Jesus is to be the focus of our lives, service, and devotion. He is to be the main love of the Church. Many things—doctrines, leaders, disputes, and traditions—occupy the thoughts of the Church and its members. When writing the study for Philippians, I pointed out that Paul mentioned Jesus' name ten times in the first 18 verses. It really is supposed to be all about Jesus, but often we have managed to make it about so many other things but Him.

Jesus is both an apostle and high priest. I have commented in other studies about the current apostolic movement, where it is recognized that apostles, literally those who are "sent forth," are still part of the Church today. Some have used this to position themselves for special honor, blessings, and financial gain. This should not be.

If anyone is an apostle, they should remember that Jesus is one Himself and consequently model their apostolic ministry after Him. Jesus wore no robes, took no title, had no reserved parking space, did not hire his family, and did not earn a large salary. The Church would be stronger if we fixed our thoughts on Jesus and not on other men and women.

3:2-3 Jesus was appointed a high priest and He was faithful to His appointment. The Jewish writer of Hebrews, writing to Jewish believers, compared Jesus to the preeminent Jewish leader, Moses. He started out mentioning that both were faithful to God's plan for their lives. That is where the comparison ended, however, for Jesus was superior to Moses. John wrote, "For the law was given through Moses; grace and truth came through Jesus Christ" (John 1:17-18).

The Jews clung to Moses and refused to follow Jesus. The Hebrews to whom this letter was written were tragically considering allegiance once again to Moses, an inferior apostle to Jesus:

> Then they hurled insults at him and said, "You are this fellow's disciple! We are disciples of

Moses! We know that God spoke to Moses, but as for this fellow, we don't even know where he comes from" (John 9:28-29).

Peter himself had been tempted to make Jesus an equal with Moses, for when he was on the mountain with Jesus, Moses and Elijah appeared to Jesus and talked with Him. Peter wanted to build a monument to all three men, but God intervened:

> Peter said to Jesus, "Lord, it is good for us to be here. If you wish, I will put up three shelters-one for you, one for Moses and one for Elijah." While he was still speaking, a bright cloud enveloped them, and a voice from the cloud said, "This is my Son, whom I love; with him I am well pleased. Listen to him!" (Matthew 17:4-5).

God's message is the same today as then: "Don't make anyone the equal of my Son. He is supreme and preeminent, and I command that you listen to Him and Him alone." **To whose voice are you listening? Is the Son supreme in your mind, work, and ministry, or are there rivals who also have significant influence in your life?**

3:4 Jesus is worthy of greater honor than Moses, Elijah, Peter, Paul, Martin Luther, any Pope, any modern-day apostle, Buddha, Mohammed, or the Dalai Lama. Jesus is Lord of all and anyone who shares Jesus' glory with another is a fool, guilty of idolatry. Jesus is on a par with no one else. He is Lord of all and Master Builder of the Church, for which He gave His life.

3:5-6 Moses was a servant in God's house but Jesus is a son. The house of which the author wrote was the Church, made up of people like you and me. Moses was a servant who helped build the house, but Jesus was the heir of the house. Moses can teach us, but our allegiance belongs to Jesus and not our church, church leader, church doctrine, church tradition, or church history.

You may read what I just wrote and nod your head, saying, "That's right. Amen, brother." Are you then guilty, however, of also saying, "Well, that's the way we've always done things in this church" or "We can't say or do things like that around here because the bishop, pastor, elder or deacons will not permit it"? It's easy to say "Amen" to a word; it's another thing to walk it out. The truth that Jesus alone is worthy of honor and praise in the Church can be difficult to walk out, as seen in the following passages:

> Then some Pharisees and teachers of the law came to Jesus from Jerusalem and asked, "Why do your disciples break the tradition of the elders? They don't wash their hands before they eat!" Jesus replied, "And why do you break the command of God for the sake of your tradition?" (Matthew 15:1-3).

> So the Pharisees and teachers of the law asked Jesus, "Why don't your disciples live according to the tradition of the elders instead of eating their food with 'unclean' hands?" He replied, "Isaiah was right when he prophesied about you hypocrites; as it is written: 'These people honor me with their lips, but their hearts are far from me. They worship me in vain; their teachings are but rules taught by men.' You have let go of the commands of God and are holding on to the traditions of men" (Mark 7:5-8).

> "Thus you nullify the word of God by your tradition that you have handed down. And you do many things like that" (Mark 7:13).

Have you nullified the word of God to follow the traditions of men? Have you looked the other way when others have done so? If you answer yes to either of those two questions, what are you going to do about it? Jesus said,

> "I do not accept praise from men, but I know you. I know that you do not have the love of God in your hearts. I have come in my Father's name, and you do not accept me; but if someone else comes in his own name, you will accept him. How can you believe if you accept praise from one another, yet make no effort to obtain the praise that comes from the only God? "But do not think I will accuse you before the Father. Your accuser is Moses, on whom your hopes are set. If you believed Moses, you would believe me, for he wrote about me. But since you do not believe what he wrote, how are you going to believe what I say?" (John 5:41-47).

Have you worked for the praise of men at the expense of God's praise? I know there are times when I have done so, and I have repented and am trying to walk out my faithfulness and loyalty to God and God alone.

> ⁷So, as the Holy Spirit says: "Today, if you hear his voice, ⁸do not harden your hearts as you did in the rebellion, during the time of testing in the desert, ⁹where your fathers tested and tried me and for forty years saw what I did. ¹⁰That is why I was angry with that generation, and I said, 'Their hearts are always going astray, and they have not known my ways.' ¹¹So I declared on oath in my anger, 'They shall never enter my rest.'"

3:7-9 The writer of Hebrews obviously believed the Holy Spirit wrote the Scriptures—here he quoted from Psalm 85:7—and that the content of the Bible is God's Word. Notice the writer did not say, "The Holy Spirit said" but rather "The Holy Spirit says." The Word is still speaking and the key word after that is "today." When I was a pastor, I would meet with some of the people with whom I worked and would usually ask, "What is the Lord saying?" I have found God is always speaking, addressing something in our lives He wants to change or an area in which He wants us to grow and mature. **What is God emphasizing in your life right now? What is the theme?**

The issue is not whether God speaks, but whether we will listen. The writer urged them not to "harden their hearts." There are many things that can harden a heart, but fear and rebellion are the two leading causes. **Are fear or rebellion working in your life right now? What could you do for God if you were not afraid?**

The Lord tested His people in the wilderness and taught them to listen to His voice. God will test you the same way to accomplish the same end:

> Remember how the Lord your God led you all the way in the desert these forty years, to humble you and to test you in order to know what was in your heart, whether or not you would keep his commands. He humbled you, causing you to hunger and then feeding you with manna, which neither you nor your fathers had known, to teach you that man does not live on bread alone but on every word that comes from the mouth of the Lord. Your clothes did not wear out and your feet did not swell during these forty years. Know then in your heart that as a man disciplines his son, so the Lord your God disciplines you (Deuteronomy 8:2-5).

Has this been your experience? Are you experiencing a time of testing now? How are you reacting to it? Is God leading you through a desert experience in your walk with Him?

3:10 It is important to worship God as He is and not as you want Him to be, for it is possible to worship a false image of God in your mind. It is important, therefore, to know God's ways and be familiar with how He will act and what He will do. You are told that Moses knew God's ways, but Israel was only familiar with God's deeds or actions: "He made known his ways to Moses, his deeds to the people of Israel" (Psalm 103:7).

I want to know God and be acquainted with His heart. I am not saying I can know everything about God, but I want to recognize His works and respond to His voice. **Will you pray the following with me?**

Lord, don't let me harden my heart. Don't permit me to keep testing You, demanding that You prove Yourself to me according to my will. You have nothing to prove to me, Lord. You have been faithful. I don't want You to disappoint or anger You, Lord, so I ask You continue to speak and help me to obey.

3:11 God made a vow when He was angry with Israel that they would not enter His rest. We want and need God's rest. To obtain it, we must do things God's way and trust Him that He is good and knows what He is doing. God put an angel to guard the entrance to the Garden of Eden so no man could enter again. In similar fashion, He put a guard over the doorway to His rest, forbidding those who have hardened their hearts from ever finding that rest until they walked again in faith. Let's move on and see precisely what it is that prevents us from entering the rest God intends us to enjoy.

¹²See to it, brothers, that none of you has a sinful, unbelieving heart that turns away from the living God. ¹³But encourage one another daily, as long as it is called Today, so that none of you may be hardened by sin's deceitfulness. ¹⁴We have come to share in Christ if we hold firmly till the end the confidence we had at first. ¹⁵As has just been said: "Today, if you hear his voice, do not harden your hearts as you did in the rebellion." ¹⁶Who were they who heard and rebelled? Were they not all those Moses led out of Egypt? ¹⁷And with whom was he angry for forty years? Was it not with those who sinned, whose bodies fell in the desert? ¹⁸And to whom did God swear that they would never enter his rest if not to those who disobeyed? ¹⁹So we see that they were not able to enter, because of their unbelief.

3:12 Faith is not a feeling. In this verse, the writer commanded that no on have a "sinful, unbelieving heart." This indicates that everyone can make the decision to have a holy, believing heart, or an unbelieving one. **What is the condition of your heart? When did your last faith testimony occur? If it occurred more than 12 months ago, why has it been so long? What are you believing the Lord for right now?**

It would seem that rest and faith, and rest and unbelief, are connected in some way. Let's read on to determine the connection.

3:13 You need the daily encouragement of other believers or at least during the "today" to which the Holy Spirit is referring. A life of faith taxes your natural inclinations because things don't happen according to your timetable or in a way you can understand. A life of faith operates according to God's plan and timing. Some people have "gotten off the faith bus" because the journey was too long, bumpy, or unpredictable. While they are good and holy people, they have decided the faith life involves too much pressure and they have subtly hardened their heart to any faith project.

3:14 Someone once said that a walk with God is not a sprint but a marathon. There are those who start fast in the Lord but fade. You must firmly hold your faith confidence from first to last and finish well in faith, just as you started. If you don't, you are in danger of not entering the rest God has for you.

It never requires less but rather more faith to make progress in the things of God. It is like raising a child. When they are babies, their parents need diaper faith. When they are older, the parents need faith for university tuition. The needs are greater, and so the faith to obtain them must be greater as well. You cannot have diaper faith and expect to receive university tuition.

3:15 The rebellion mentioned in this verse is from Psalm 95, quoted for the second time in this chapter, and is a description of the events that occurred in Exodus 16 and 17. It was there that the people murmured against the Lord for what they perceived to be His lack of provision. They considered going back to Egypt because they did not like their living conditions and they did not trust the Lord for anything better. The people provoked the Lord and He threatened to let them die there, and they would have, had it not been for Moses' intervention.

The rebellion described here was an issue of faith in the hearts of the people. They had decided not to go on in faith, but rather to take matters into their own hands. Even though they had seen great things, they wearied and hardened their hearts. **Have you seen God do great things for you, but are you in the same place? Are you tired of the faith journey, and considering turning back?** The message to you is the same as it was to the original readers of this letter: Don't do it.

3:16-17 Only Joshua and Caleb who were present at the rebellion made it to the Promised Land. A lot of people died because of their disobedience. When you think of their fate, consider what Jesus said:

> Someone asked him, "Lord, are only a few people going to be saved?" He said to them, "Make every effort to enter through the narrow door, because many, I tell you, will try to enter and will not be able to" (Luke 13:23-24).

Just because someone talks about the Lord or attends church doesn't mean they will fully enter into all that God has for them. **Are you committed to seeing your faith journey through to its successful completion?**

3:18-19 They did not enter rest because they disobeyed, and their disobedience took the form of unbelief. It seems then that disobedience and unbelief are one and the same. If you hear and don't act on what you hear, then you are exercising disobedience, which is a manifestation of unbelief. It is safe to conclude that faith and obedience lead to rest, even though they may cause you to be more active than disobedience. We can also conclude that rest isn't a cessation of activities, but rather a proper attitude and perspective in the midst of activities. That attitude is one of quiet confidence in the God who is leading and providing for you.

Do you have rest now? Are you at peace, even if you are experiencing lack or hard times where work, ministry, and family are concerned? I keep a busy schedule, but I have learned to rest in Him while I am on the go. That enables me to enjoy His rest even while I am active. This verse is not referring to a literal Sabbath day, although I do think we all need to plan for a day off for worship and to do things that give us refreshment (even God took a day off after six days of creation). The rest the writer was talking about here was not a literal day, but rather an attitude that God is in control, so you can trust Him for all you need and for the outcome of all your faith ventures.

4

Therefore, since the promise of entering his rest still stands, let us be careful that none of you be found to have fallen short of it. ²For we also have had the gospel preached to us, just as they did; but the message they heard was of no value to them, because those who heard did not combine it with faith. ³Now we who have believed enter that rest, just as God has said, "So I declared on oath in my anger, 'They shall never enter my rest.'" And yet his work has been finished since the creation of the world. ⁴For somewhere he has spoken about the seventh day in these words: "And on the seventh day God rested from all his work." ⁵And again in the passage above he says, "They shall never enter my rest."

4:1-3 Faith is our means to spiritual and physical rest. Our faith-rest is not only spiritual but also physical because anxiety and worry take their toll on our bodies and minds. When we trust God for our salvation, provision, and protection we can rest in the fact that He neither slumbers nor sleeps. He is able to do what He said He would do. **How did Israel come short of entering the rest God had for them?**

> That night all the people of the community raised their voices and wept aloud. All the Israelites grumbled against Moses and Aaron, and the whole assembly said to them, "If only we had died in Egypt! Or in this desert! Why is the Lord bringing us to this land only to let us fall by the sword? Our wives and children will be taken as plunder. Wouldn't it be better for us to go back to Egypt?" And they said to each other, "We should choose a leader and go back to Egypt."
>
> Then Moses and Aaron fell facedown in front of the whole Israelite assembly gathered there. Joshua son of Nun and Caleb son of Jephunneh, who were among those who had explored the land, tore their clothes and said to the entire Israelite assembly, "The land we passed through and explored is exceedingly good. If the Lord is pleased with us, he will lead us into that land, a land flowing with milk and honey, and will give it to us. Only do not rebel against the Lord. And do not be afraid of the people of the land, because we will swallow them up. Their protection is gone, but the Lord is with us. Do not be afraid of them" (Numbers 14:1-9).

The writer was exhorting the believing Hebrews not to imitate their ancestors by not entering the Promised Land. They did not go in because they did not trust in God. The same exhortation goes out to us. **Are you disillusioned with your** walk with the Lord? Has it been harder than you thought it would be? Have you stopped your faith journey, content to talk about God intellectually but not experientially? Is the sum total of your walk going to church on Sunday?

4:4-5 God entered rest from His own works but vowed that Israel would not rest from their works when they refused to believe. In Jesus' day, the Jews had perfected a system of works that would have made many tired. They were actually exhilarated by their religious system and defended it against any who opposed it, even Jesus Himself. **Have you ever considered that the Jews had to kill God to preserve their system of worshiping God?**

Do you have a system so religious even God cannot penetrate it? If so, you haven't entered the rest God has for you. If you persist, He will make sure you never enter it.

> [6]It still remains that some will enter that rest, and those who formerly had the gospel preached to them did not go in, because of their disobedience. [7]Therefore God again set a certain day, calling it Today, when a long time later he spoke through David, as was said before: "Today, if you hear his voice, do not harden your hearts." [8]For if Joshua had given them rest, God would not have spoken later about another day. [9]There remains, then, a Sabbath-rest for the people of God; [10]for anyone who enters God's rest also rests from his own work, just as God did from his. [11]Let us, therefore, make every effort to enter that rest, so that no one will fall by following their example of disobedience.

4:6 The writer stated that those in the Old Testament had "the gospel" preached to them. Remember that gospel simply means "good news." They had the good news but could not receive it because they were disobedient and without faith. It seems that nothing has changed, for there are some today who have the good news presented to them, but they reject it, or have it and don't do anything with it—their lives are unchanged and unfazed. **What is the issue?** The issue is always faith, for without faith, it is impossible to please God, as we shall later in Hebrews 11.

Does it surprise you that the Old Testament "saints" had the gospel preached to them? When I first realized that, it surprised me, for I thought the gospel was an exclusive New Testament entity. Paul also wrote about this truth to the Corinthians:

> For I do not want you to be ignorant of the fact, brothers and sisters, that *our ancestors* were all under the cloud and that they all passed through the sea. They were all baptized into Moses in the cloud and in the sea. They all ate the same spiritual food and drank the same spiritual drink; for they drank from the spiritual rock that accompanied them, and that rock was Christ. Nevertheless, God was not pleased with most of them; their bodies were scattered in the wilderness (1 Corinthians 10:1-5, emphasis added).

Paul referred to the Jews in the wilderness as "our ancestors," and he included the Corinthians in the "our." In other words, the Jews of old, the Hebrew readers, and the Corinthians were all part of the same movement, the Church if you will. That means they all had the gospel preached to them, just as this verse in Hebrews indicates. What's more, we are part of the "our," grafted into the family of God through the gospel, which is faith in Christ.

4:7 This is the third time the word "today" was referenced in this letter. God is a "today God." God sets certain days to do certain things in certain lives. **What is your "today" at this time? What is the season you are in? Do you know? Are you being obedient and full of faith?**

My today is writing and publishing. My yesterday was being a pastor and traveling with a worship team to conduct seminars and concerts. If I live and the Lord tarries, I will have other todays. Don't miss your today by focusing on yesterday or tomorrow. The best thing you can do in your walk with the Lord is to obey Him today and trust Him for tomorrow. **What is your today?**

4:8-11 This is an unusual statement: Let us make every "effort" to enter that rest. We must work to rest, which seems like an oxymoron: We must exert energy to rest. Spiritual rest—resting in God—doesn't just happen. We must obey and work to maintain our obedience. We must cease from our own work and then embrace the deeds and work God has for us. Keep in mind what Paul wrote to the Ephesians: "For we are God's handiwork, created in Christ Jesus to do good works, which God prepared in advance for us to do" (Ephesians 2:10).

God has works for us to do, but those works are not to earn our standing with God. They are to confirm the reality of our standing with God. Remember, this letter was written to Jews who were accustomed to a busy schedule of God-works at the Feasts and the Temple. Then a Jewish believer and preacher was writing to tell them that Moses, Joshua, and David did not lead God's people to true rest. It was only in the gospel of Jesus that their rest could be found.

These Jews were considering "going back" to Judaism, but the writer was equating that with unbelief and disobedience. **Are you considering "going back"? Did you begin your walk with Jesus in faith, only to find it difficult? Are you disillusioned that some promises have lingered and some things of God require too much time and effort?** If you answer yes, then maybe it's time to rest from trying to "figure things out." Maybe it's simply time to rest from your labors and enter into the rest that God has for you. Perhaps some people have advised you over the years to just "give it to the Lord." Perhaps this is what they meant—just trust God for the results while you work to carry out His plans for you.

> ¹²For the word of God is living and active. Sharper than any double-edged sword, it penetrates even to dividing soul and spirit, joints and marrow; it judges the thoughts and attitudes of the heart. ¹³Nothing in all creation is hidden from God's sight. Everything is uncovered and laid bare before the eyes of him to whom we must give account. ¹⁴Therefore, since we have a great high priest who has gone through the heavens, Jesus the Son of God, let us hold firmly to the faith we profess. ¹⁵For we do not have a high priest who is unable to sympathize with our weaknesses, but we have one who has been tempted in every way, just as we are-yet was without sin. ¹⁶Let us then approach the throne of grace with confidence, so that we may receive mercy and find grace to help us in our time of need.

4:12

Someone once said that the Bible is the oldest book whose author is still alive. There is a living God backing up His word, and that is why the word of God is also living and active. I am always in awe of the Bible's ability to judge what I am thinking today. The Bible can evaluate whether I love my wife or if I am doing a good job at work—even though written thousands of years ago.

The Bible contains history, but it is not a history book; science, but its focus isn't science. The Bible is a book about a good God seeking wayward people, and then giving those people a standard by which they are to conduct their lives. When these same people confess they are not able to maintain that standard, then God comes and lives in them to enable them to keep His "rules." This is how magnificent our God is. His word is an active agent able to penetrate the hardest heart and darkest places. When it penetrates the darkness, His Spirit comes to bring and maintain light.

We should not read the Bible just to be familiar with its stories and themes. We should read it so it can change us into the people God wants us to be. We read the Word to get the Word in us so it can do the work that needs to be done so desperately in our minds, lives, and hearts:

> How can a young man keep his way pure? By living according to your word. I seek you with all my heart; do not let me stray from your commands. I have hidden your word in my heart that I might not sin against you (Psalm 119:9-11).

Psalm 119 is the longest psalm and takes some time to read, but it may be worth your while to read it today or this week. It is located exactly at the midpoint of the Bible, and is the pivot point upon which the entire Word rests, sort of like the fulcrum of a seesaw. From Psalm 119, you can "swing" back to the Old or forward to the New Testament, but both Testaments are one and the same—they are God's word to man.

4:13 God sees it all and that's why I am always surprised that people are not more honest with God. They act like they will tell God something He doesn't know or that will make Him angry. If God were going to "get you," He would have "gotten" you already. **If God knows your thoughts and words before you say them, then why would saying them make God angry?** My point is that you can be honest with God. Everyone must give Him an account of their life, whether now or later. I want to do mine now and ask His forgiveness where and when I need it.

Is there anything you need to tell God today? Are you clear that He already knows and that this is for your benefit and not His? If you need further convincing, then read some of the psalms and see some of the brutal honesty the writers applied when talking with the Lord.

4:14-16 We are introduced to the theme of Jesus' High Priestly ministry in this verse. As the high priest went through the tabernacle and Temple to the Holy of Holies, Jesus went through the heavens. He fulfilled God's desire for righteousness in a spiritual sense and, because He did, we can hold fast our confession of faith in Him and His priestly work.

Jesus is a human being, just like you and me. He understands us not simply because He created us, but because He is one of us, in every way except sin. The Greek gods were bizarre and toyed with people, teasing them and then punishing them according to the gods' whims. Modern gods are no different. The god of Islam is so far away that there is no hope anyone can know or touch him. The Buddhist god lies within every man and has a million different faces, all of which take on the look of the people who "carry" that god. But our God, the God of heaven and earth, is one of us. We can go to Him because He understands. He may rebuke or discipline, but He understands and empathizes with our plight.

As a pastor I knew once said, our flesh sits on the throne in heaven. We are well represented in the heavens, so go there with confidence, expecting help and not judgment.

5

Every high priest is selected from among men and is appointed to represent them in matters related to God, to offer gifts and sacrifices for sins. ²He is able to deal gently with those who are ignorant and are going astray, since he himself is subject to weakness. ³This is why he has to offer sacrifices for his own sins, as well as for the sins of the people. ⁴No one takes this honor upon himself; he must be called by God, just as Aaron was.

5:1 There is still a mentality in many that there should be certain men (or women) who do the "things of God" while everyone else goes about their daily business. That all changed, however, with Jesus. He was the great High Priest and thus, we are all priests today, having access to God and permitted to relate to God directly rather than through a priestly caste or mediator:

> But you are a chosen people, *a royal priesthood,* a holy nation, a people belonging to God, that you may declare the praises of him who called you

out of darkness into his wonderful light (1 Peter 2:9-10, emphasis added).

5:2-3 All priests in the old covenant were sinners themselves and made sacrifices for their own sins as well as the people's. They were supposed to be mindful of man's sinful condition so they could deal gently with others. This rule still applies today:

> Brothers, if someone is caught in a sin, you who are spiritual should restore him gently. But watch yourself, or you also may be tempted. Carry each other's burdens, and in this way you will fulfill the law of Christ. If anyone thinks he is something when he is nothing, he deceives himself. Each one should test his own actions. Then he can take pride in himself, without comparing himself to somebody else, for each one should carry his own load (Galatians 6:1-5).

Martin Luther spoke of and helped restore what he called the "priesthood of the believer." As "priests," we are to be mindful of our own condition, thus having grace and mercy for the similar condition in others.

5:4 It is an honor to do God's work, an honor now available to *all* believers. We do not choose it; we are chosen for it. First, Aaron was chosen to be Moses' spokesperson, then he was chosen to be a priest. **Do you see yourself as a priest of God? Are you comfortable with that title and role? How do you carry out your priestly duties?** (Prayer, witnessing, reading the Word, and fulfilling your purpose wherever you are called are a few ways that come to mind.) **How can you be a more effective priest?**

⁵So Christ also did not take upon

> himself the glory of becoming a high priest. But God said to him, "You are my Son; today I have become your Father." ⁶And he says in another place, "You are a priest forever, in the order of Melchizedek." ⁷During the days of Jesus' life on earth, he offered up prayers and petitions with loud cries and tears to the one who could save him from death, and he was heard because of his reverent submission. ⁸Although he was a son, he learned obedience from what he suffered ⁹and, once made perfect, he became the source of eternal salvation for all who obey him ¹⁰and was designated by God to be high priest in the order of Melchizedek.

5:5 Since Jesus was not a Levite—He was of the tribe of Judah—He was not of the priestly family of Aaron. Therefore, He did not claim the High Priest's office by means of birth, but through an appointment by God. Here the writer quoted Psalm 2:7, which he had also referred to in Hebrews 1:5. There was an important connection between Christ's Son-ship and His role as High Priest.

5:6 The writer then quoted Psalm 110:4 and positioned that verse as a Messianic reference. Jesus did not use the title "High Priest," nor did anyone use this title while referring to Him. His priesthood was not in line with Aaron's, but rather modeled after Melchizedek. Since the writer continued this thought later in the letter, we will discuss Melchizedek then too. Suffice it to say now that Jesus was an eternal priest whose ministry was different than that of the high priests Israel had previously known.

5:7 The picture painted here is a powerful one. Jesus did not rely on His divinity to achieve His mission. He was a priest and functioned as such out of His humanity, which included a vibrant prayer life:

> He withdrew about a stone's throw beyond them, knelt down and prayed, "Father, if you are willing, take this cup from me; yet not my will, but yours be done." An angel from heaven appeared to him and strengthened him. And being in anguish, he prayed more earnestly, and his sweat was like drops of blood falling to the ground (Luke 22:41-44).

It is said in Luke 22:41 that Jesus withdrew a "stone's throw" from the disciples to pray. Why? Perhaps because He was so noisy when He prayed. Jesus did not pray solemn, polite prayers, nor did He say "in Jesus' name" at the end of His prayers. When Jesus prayed, He talked to His Father out of His suffering and pain. Jesus was heard, not because He was God, but because He knew how to "get hold of God."

It is my theory that when Jesus sweat blood, He had done that before. He was accustomed to praying so fervently that the blood vessels in His forehead burst and mixed blood with sweat. You don't have that happen by praying what I call "Now-I-lay-me-down-to-sleep" prayers. Jesus was fervent when He prayed, expressing His urgent need for His Father's help.

I have adjusted my own prayer life based on this image of how Jesus prayed. You would be wise to do the same. **Are you a fervent or polite pray-er? How can you make your prayer life more meaningful and effective? Are you happy with your answers to prayer?**

> [8] Although he was a son, he learned

obedience from what he suffered ⁹and, once made perfect, he became the source of eternal salvation for all who obey him ¹⁰and was designated by God to be high priest in the order of Melchizedek.

5:8 In Philippians, there is a powerful description of Jesus referred to as the "kenotic" passage (kenosis is the Greek word for "emptying"):

> Your attitude should be the same as that of Christ Jesus: Who, being in very nature God, did not consider equality with God something to be grasped, but made himself nothing [emptied himself], taking the very nature of a servant, being made in human likeness. And being found in appearance as a man, he humbled himself and became obedient to death—even death on a cross (Philippians 2:5-8)!

It is hard to imagine that Jesus would learn anything since He was the epitome of perfection. Even a master violinist can become better, however, even though there was no imperfection prior to the improvement. That violinist can improve with age as he or she learns new techniques or learns how to present the music more effectively.

If Jesus learned obedience through His suffering, how do you think you and I will learn? Will it be by a different path? Where are you suffering right now and what are you learning in the midst of it?

5:9 The word for "perfect" here is one that is used to describe someone who has reached their goal. Jesus became complete when He died and was raised from the dead and is now a source of salvation for all. For anyone to receive the benefit of this salvation, however, they must obey Him, not just believe in Him or talk about Him.

5:10 Jesus wasn't a priest in the past tense. He is a priest, still functioning in His priestly role according to God's will and serving on behalf of anyone who has faith in and obeys Him.

> ¹¹We have much to say about this, but it is hard to explain because you are slow to learn. ¹²In fact, though by this time you ought to be teachers, you need someone to teach you the elementary truths of God's word all over again. You need milk, not solid food! ¹³Anyone who lives on milk, being still an infant, is not acquainted with the teaching about righteousness. ¹⁴But solid food is for the mature, who by constant use have trained themselves to distinguish good from evil.

5:11 The Hebrew readers were rebuked for their slowness to learn, for they should have been progressing in their understanding of Jesus. Instead, they were bogged down by their romantic and cultural connection to Judaism. Tradition can keep us from growing in God. The Jewish writer who wrote this letter was himself growing in his understanding of Scripture and Jesus. The Jews to whom he was writing were not growing. **Has loyalty to any tradition—church or otherwise—hindered the growth of your faith? Are you walking out your faith or your adherence to certain doctrines? If so, what are you prepared to do about it?**

5:12-13 The truth in this verse holds true even today. The baby-boomer generation has had more Bible teaching than any previous generation. We have more Bible translations, teaching program, videos, books, and church classes than at any point in history. Yet we have few who are willing to teach the elementary truths. Believers are often fed every week, indeed every day, but are somehow stunted in their spiritual growth, and incapable of sharing what they know with others.

5:14 In 1987, I enrolled in a class called "Systematic Theology." I enjoyed the class, but I was troubled by it as well. I had been a pastor for 13 years at that point, but I was hearing things in class I had never heard before. I was ignorant and not growing in doctrine, church history, or biblical studies. Even though I had neither the time nor money, I kept going back to school and eventually earned my doctorate nine years later.

During that time, I tried to learn to distinguish between good and evil, the special and the ordinary, the holy and the profane. I am still learning. I am writing these studies in part to continue to grow as a writer and teacher. I want solid food; I don't want to live on milk, which could be my past experiences or the titles that have been bestowed on me as I grow older.

Are you growing in your knowledge of your faith? Are you progressing to food and away from baby's milk where faith is concerned? Are you growing in your ability to discuss and explain your faith? If the answer is no to any of those questions, what are you prepared to do about it? What options are available to you?

6

> Therefore let us leave the elementary teachings about Christ and go on to maturity, not laying again the foundation of repentance from acts that lead to death, and of faith in God, ²instruction about baptisms, the laying on of hands, the resurrection of the dead, and eternal judgment. ³And God permitting, we will do so.

6:1-2 The writer considered repentance, faith, baptisms, laying on of hands, the resurrection, and eternal judgment to be elementary teachings. **How much do you know about each of those six topics? Can you explain them? Can you point out biblical references that address those topics?** It would make a good study and warrants investing time to study and know the basics of each topic.

Often in sports, the most successful players are those who master the fundamentals, going on to outstanding performance. The same is true for those who are following Jesus. I went back to school in 1987 to earn my doctorate because I wasn't happy with my lack of understanding of basic theological issues. That ignorance was not going to disappear unless I addressed it. Then I went back to school in 2007 for another degree. **What situation are you hoping will disappear, but will not unless you take specific, corrective steps?** My ignorance of biblical matters was not going to disappear. I had to take steps to alleviate it.

6:3 Remember, these Hebrews were considering abandoning the faith to return to Judaism. They would have had to turn their backs on these elementary teachings to embrace all kinds of acts that led to death. Modern Christians can do the same thing and return to their former way of life when faith in Christ becomes too uncomfortable. I urge you to continue to grow in the grace and the knowledge of God, not tiring of the journey or disillusioned by disappointments:

> And we pray this in order that you may live a life worthy of the Lord and may please him in every way: bearing fruit in every good work, growing in the knowledge of God, being strengthened with all power according to his glorious might so that you may have great endurance and patience, and joyfully giving thanks to the Father, who has qualified you to share in the inheritance of the saints in the kingdom of light. For he has rescued us from the dominion of darkness and brought us into the kingdom of the Son he loves, in whom we have redemption, the forgiveness of sins (Colossians 1:10-14).
>
> On hearing it, many of his disciples said, "This is a hard teaching. Who can accept it?" Aware that his disciples were grumbling about this, Jesus said to them, "Does this offend you? What

> if you see the Son of Man ascend to where he was before! The Spirit gives life; the flesh counts for nothing. The words I have spoken to you are spirit and they are life. Yet there are some of you who do not believe." For Jesus had known from the beginning which of them did not believe and who would betray him. He went on to say, "This is why I told you that no one can come to me unless the Father has enabled him." From this time many of his disciples turned back and no longer followed him. "You do not want to leave too, do you?" Jesus asked the Twelve. Simon Peter answered him, "Lord, to whom shall we go? You have the words of eternal life. We believe and know that you are the Holy One of God." (John 6:60-69).

I have seen some people who I admired because of the vibrancy of their faith return to their roots as they got older. They went back to their denominational heritage instead of continuing to blaze new faith trails in their lives for others to follow. I am not judging them; I am only comparing what they did to what these believing Jews were considering. These Jews wanted to "go back," and some of my friends went back too, content to follow the familiar rules of their upbringing instead of walking in the Spirit as they once had. This makes me think of what was written later in Hebrews:

> All these people were still living by faith when they died. They did not receive the things promised; they only saw them and welcomed them from a distance, admitting that they were foreigners and strangers on earth. People who say such things show that they are looking for a

country of their own. If they had been thinking of the country they had left, *they would have had opportunity to return.* Instead, they were longing for a better country—a heavenly one. Therefore God is not ashamed to be called their God, for he has prepared a city for them (Hebrews 11:13-16, emphasis added).

The concept here is that they were looking to return or go back. In a sense, my friends went back too, looking for comfort in their old ways. I have prayed, *Lord, I don't want to go back. I want to be led by the Spirit until I die. I have nothing to 'go back' to that compares to what I have in you today.*

> ⁴It is impossible for those who have once been enlightened, who have tasted the heavenly gift, who have shared in the Holy Spirit, ⁵who have tasted the goodness of the word of God and the powers of the coming age, ⁶if they fall away, to be brought back to repentance, because to their loss they are crucifying the Son of God all over again and subjecting him to public disgrace. ⁷Land that drinks in the rain often falling on it and that produces a crop useful to those for whom it is farmed receives the blessing of God. ⁸But land that produces thorns and thistles is worthless and is in danger of being cursed. In the end it will be burned.

6:4-6 There is always an intense debate over whether or not someone can lose their salvation. Here we see that someone can give it back. The writer was not addressing someone who had sinned or made a grievous error. The writer was talking to people who were considering a rational, calculated decision to depart from the Way and return to Judaism. Someone who would do this could not be reinstated to life in Christ, according to the author.

Verse six summarized what someone was doing who denied Jesus, having once known Him: they were crucifying Him all over again. We know that the Father had Jesus suffer and die once and only once. Anyone who would deny Christ after having known Him is a "Christ-killer," rendering His love and grace useless and embracing a counterfeit after having known the real. For that, there can be little help from God. He gave His Son; there is nothing more He can do.

The postmodern mindset is that sincerity is the most important component of seeking God. If someone is sincere, there can be many ways to God. And what could be more sincere and meaningful than a return to Judaism, from which much of Jesus' teaching came? Certainly that would not be a bad thing? Yet the writer of Hebrews was clear: Jesus was and is superior to Judaism. A return to Judaism once someone was a Christian was a fatal error, and the writer was doing all he (or they) could to prevent this from happening.

To choose a path apart from Christ when someone has seen and experienced Christ was and is folly. It is man determining for himself what is in his best interests. The writer was making a passionate appeal that Christ was and is the answer, the only answer for the lostness of man. Judaism was good to a point, but has been superseded by faith in Christ.

Do you believe Christ is the only way to God? The writer of this letter certainly did and did not see Judaism as an acceptable alternative. If this writer, who was a contemporary to the move of God in the early days, didn't see Judaism or any other alternative as an option, then we should not either.

Have you encountered hardships in your life and ministry? Have you "cooled" to the cause of Christ because you are disillusioned or hurt? If so, I implore you not to turn your back on Jesus. Press through your pain and sorrow and reassess whether idealism or a wrong concept of who Jesus is or what Jesus did or did not do caused you to become angry and lose heart. Then reconsider the great treasure you have in Jesus, even if your life has not turned out the way you thought it would. He is still worthy of all praise and honor.

6:7-8 These two verses are part of my list of personal governing values—those things that motivate me to action in my life. This particular governing value states,

> **I am productive** – The root word of executive is "execute." It's not enough to be busy, but I must execute correct plans and procedures that will produce the desired fruit and results. The writer of Hebrews cautioned us not just to drink in the goodness of God, then produce no results from that goodness. I want to produce more than I use and engage in activities that will bring increase and glory to God and provide a good example of faith to those with whom I work.

> **Do you have a set of governing values?** If not, go to my website, read my values article there, and then develop your own values. It's a simple process and will bear fruit for many years to come. I use these values to hold myself accountable to do those things I claim are most important to me.

> **Are you as productive as you would like to be?**

As you need to be? Are you busy with things that matter and are most important to you? To recapture your time and life isn't impossible, but it will take effort and commitment. Once you develop your values, activities related to those values must show up in two important places: your checkbook and your calendar. If you are doing things not connected to those personal values, then you must consider how to stop doing them.

> [9] Even though we speak like this, dear friends, we are confident of better things in your case-things that accompany salvation. [10] God is not unjust; he will not forget your work and the love you have shown him as you have helped his people and continue to help them. [11] We want each of you to show this same diligence to the very end, in order to make your hope sure. [12] We do not want you to become lazy, but to imitate those who through faith and patience inherit what has been promised.

6:9 The author at this point employed a more conciliatory tone, having confronted the readers with stern words about the possibility of leaving the faith. This reminded me of what Paul wrote to the Romans:

> Consider therefore the kindness and sternness of God: sternness to those who fell, but kindness to you, provided that you continue in his kindness. Otherwise, you also will be cut off (Romans 11:22-23).

The writer was confident the Hebrew readers would enjoy and walk in the things that accompany the saving message of Jesus and not the things that go with dead doctrines. His confidence was in the God who would preserve them, unless of course those in need of help refused God's assistance.

6:10 God is not unjust. He will not forget your work and love for His people. Dear reader, if you are discouraged today, I urge you to take these words to heart. God hasn't forgotten you. He is watching and has recorded all you have done for Him and His people. You *will* be rewarded. I have often said that God has a big book and a sharp pencil, and He has "written down" everything so He will remember to reward you. If you have trouble seeing this, then read the story of Mordecai:

> That night the king could not sleep; so he ordered the book of the chronicles, the record of his reign, to be brought in and read to him. It was found recorded there that Mordecai had exposed Bigthana and Teresh, two of the king's officers who guarded the doorway, who had conspired to assassinate King Xerxes. "What honor and recognition has Mordecai received for this?" the king asked. "Nothing has been done for him," his attendants answered. The king said, "Who is in the court?" Now Haman had just entered the outer court of the palace to speak to the king about hanging Mordecai on the gallows he had erected for him. His attendants answered, "Haman is standing in the court." "Bring him in," the king ordered. When Haman entered, the king asked him, "What should be done for the man the king delights to honor?" Now Haman thought to himself, "Who is there that the king would rather honor than me?" So he answered the king, "For the man the king delights to

honor, have them bring a royal robe the king has worn and a horse the king has ridden, one with a royal crest placed on its head. Then let the robe and horse be entrusted to one of the king's most noble princes. Let them robe the man the king delights to honor, and lead him on the horse through the city streets, proclaiming before him, 'This is what is done for the man the king delights to honor!'" "Go at once," the king commanded Haman. "Get the robe and the horse and do just as you have suggested for Mordecai the Jew, who sits at the king's gate. Do not neglect anything you have recommended." So Haman got the robe and the horse. He robed Mordecai, and led him on horseback through the city streets, proclaiming before him, "This is what is done for the man the king delights to honor!" (Esther 6:1-11).

One day, when you least expect it, God will reward you for your faithful service. Be encouraged today! **Are you battling discouragement? What will you do to overcome it?** I hope you will take my advice and not give up.

6:11-12 You need faith and patience to inherit what God has promised you. You must not become lazy but remain diligent. In another letter, Paul wrote, "Let us not become weary in doing good, for at the proper time we will reap a harvest if we do not give up" (Galatians 6:9).

The writer urged us to imitate those who did what he was instructing us to do. That is why we should read the life stories of those who had faith and endured. That is also why we need to hear testimonies of those who had faith and were rewarded. **Have you become lazy? Discouraged?** Then stir yourself to action and continue doing the good deeds you once did. Do not lose your trust that God will reward you.

> ¹³When God made his promise to Abraham, since there was no one greater for him to swear by, he swore by himself, ¹⁴saying, "I will surely bless you and give you many descendants." ¹⁵And so after waiting patiently, Abraham received what was promised. ¹⁶Men swear by someone greater than themselves, and the oath confirms what is said and puts an end to all argument.

6:13 In the previous verse, we were urged to learn from those who had obtained God's promises through faith and patience. In this verse, we are specifically directed to consider Abraham. While church history can provide many examples of faith and endurance, the Bible still provides the best examples. **Did you know that it is possible to be mentored and coached by a biblical character?**

If you are attracted to a certain person in the Bible, there is a reason you are. Read everything the Bible says about them, then read what the commentaries say. During your times of meditation, visualize those characters and let them "speak" to your particular situation, ministry, or crisis. You will begin to think and act like them because the Spirit, who is present in your life, was present in their lives to make them the people you are studying.

Who are your heroes in the Bible? Why not consider a comprehensive study of those characters, no matter how long it takes? When you do this, in some sense they will actually mentor you, for God will use them to shape you into the person He wants you to be.

6:14 God swore an oath by Himself since there was no one greater by which He could swear. It is of note that Abraham did not seek the promise; God approached him to bestow on him the promise. Everything begins and ends with God. The same is true for Joseph, Moses, Samuel, and David. Once the promise from God came, however, their lives were changed and they were tested beyond what they probably imagined possible.

Do you have promises God has made to you? Then be prepared to be tested as well. **Are you being tested now?** Then be encouraged and study the examples of others in the Bible who were tested and endured.

6:15 Abraham couldn't do anything but wait. The writer does not mention the instance when Abraham did not wait, that being when he took his wife's maid Hagar and got her pregnant. That decision has had a great impact on history, for the son of that liaison, Ishmael, is the father of the Arabs, enemies of the Jews. I have a friend who wrote a song with a line that states, "There's only one thing worse than waiting on God and that's wishing that you did, wishing that you did."

Are you waiting on the Lord? What are you doing while you wait? I trust you are getting ready for when the promise becomes reality so you can handle and enjoy it. The time to prepare for a promise is *before* it is fulfilled, not *when* it is fulfilled.

6:16 I don't utter oaths, so this verse is a bit hard for me to understand. I have seen people vow ("I swear to God") and be lying through their teeth. I have almost always seen their lies exposed, come to think of it. So if you do swear in the name of God, be careful. God is listening.

[17]Because God wanted to make the

unchanging nature of his purpose very clear to the heirs of what was promised, he confirmed it with an oath. [18]God did this so that, by two unchangeable things in which it is impossible for God to lie, we who have fled to take hold of the hope offered to us may be greatly encouraged. [19]We have this hope as an anchor for the soul, firm and secure. It enters the inner sanctuary behind the curtain, [20]where Jesus, who went before us, has entered on our behalf. He has become a high priest forever, in the order of Melchizedek.

6:17

God promised that all the nations of the earth would be blessed through Abraham and He confirmed that promise with an oath. God wanted to impress Abraham's heirs with the solemnity of His vow:

> "As the rain and the snow come down from heaven, and do not return to it without watering the earth and making it bud and flourish, so that it yields seed for the sower and bread for the eater, so is my word that goes out from my mouth: It will not return to me empty, but will accomplish what I desire and achieve the purpose for which I sent it" (Isaiah 55:10-11).

When God spoke to Abraham, there was no written record of His previous work to which Abraham could refer. Abraham could only take God at His word when God vowed that what He said was true. That is a pattern for us to follow. While we now have God's written word, God personally backs up His word. Our faith isn't in what God said, but it is in the God who said it. He will do what He said He will do.

6:18 The two unchangeable things mentioned here are God's promise and His oath. If God had sworn by the heavens and earth, the heavens and earth will pass away so it could be implied that the oath could be broken. Instead, God swore by Himself—and not His creation that will pass away—and since He lives forever, God is able to oversee His promises without any hindrance. We can put our trust in Him because He is able to do what He said He will do.

Even though we must wait to see the promises of God, we can still be encouraged. If something isn't happening according to our timetable, it isn't because God can't perform it; it is because God chooses not to do so at this time. That is why we are urged to trust Him. As the old hymn states, He may not come when you call Him, but He always comes on time.

6:19 The hymn "On Christ the Solid Rock I Stand" has a great line in one of the verses: "In every high and stormy gale, my anchor holds within the veil." The veil is a reference to the natural veil that separated the Holy of Holies from the rest of the tabernacle and temple. There was a similar veil between heaven and earth, but Jesus removed that veil, symbolized by the veil of the Temple ripping apart when Jesus died (see Matthew 27:51).

After the way to heaven was opened, Jesus took His place behind where that heavenly veil had been to sit at the right hand of the Father and watch over the work He had accomplished. No one can ever re-hang that curtain or veil. It is torn down forever and we have access to God because Jesus is our anchor that holds and stands behind the veil of heaven. Thank You, Jesus.

6:20 As the high priest went behind the veil once a year to offer the blood of forgiveness in the tabernacle and the Temple, Jesus now "lives" behind the veil that once existed between heaven and earth. He is perfectly doing the work that the earthly high priests had done imperfectly and irregularly. Jesus is the great High Priest, always making intercession "behind the veil" on behalf of those who are His. Our anchor does indeed hold behind the veil, not because of what we have done, but because of the blood of Jesus.

Are you living in the full assurance that Jesus lives in heaven interceding for you and yours? Be encouraged today by this vivid picture of reality.

7

> This Melchizedek was king of Salem and priest of God Most High. He met Abraham returning from the defeat of the kings and blessed him, ²and Abraham gave him a tenth of everything. First, his name means "king of righteousness"; then also, "king of Salem" means "king of peace." ³Without father or mother, without genealogy, without beginning of days or end of life, like the Son of God he remains a priest forever.

7:1 Here we see the name Melchizedek mentioned once again after a brief mention earlier in the letter. There is only a brief story involving Melchizedek in the early chapters of Genesis, so it is somewhat surprising that he should receive so much attention in this letter:

> Then Melchizedek king of Salem brought out bread and wine. He was priest of God Most High, and he blessed Abram, saying, "Blessed be Abram by God Most High, Creator of heaven and earth. And blessed be God Most High, who

delivered your enemies into your hand." Then Abram gave him a tenth of everything (Genesis 14:18-20).

This is a textbook case of Scripture interpreting Scripture, which is always the most reliable way to understand what the Spirit intended when He inspired the writers. Most believe Salem was the region or city of Jerusalem. Melchizedek was a priest; how he became a priest and who appointed him is unclear. He simply appeared on the scene and blessed God's man Abraham (see Genesis 14:18-20).

7:2 Abraham tithed from his spoils of battle to Melchizedek. Some say that tithing is Old Testament and part of the Law. Abraham predated the Law, however, and he tithed. And it is interesting that the writer of Hebrews did not comment that the tithe no longer applies to God's people. If it predated the Law, then there is a good chance that is should continue after the Law as well—or so some teach. They also usually teach that the tithe belongs in the "storehouse," which they define to be the local church.

Then there are others who maintain that the tithe belonged to the Old Testament and has no place in the New. Giving is directed by the Spirit who may direct believers to give any amount. The tithe can serve as a general guideline, but is not to be enforced literally or legalistically. This commentary is not a study of the tithe, so you can research more on this subject if it interests you.

Melchizedek had multiple titles, just like Jesus did. When I tithe, I tithe to Jesus, not to my church. I am giving to honor Him for who He is, not to get some heavenly goodies. And I am certainly not giving to avoid God's wrath. At times, some churches make the tithe sounds like protection money paid to some spiritual mafia, who say, "Pay us or

God will break your legs." I tithe because God is glorious and I *want* to do it, not because I *have* to do it to protect myself from heaven's wrath.

What is your strategy or philosphy for giving? If it is not tithing, then what is it? If you don't have a philosophy for giving, you will be dependent on your circumstances and that will cause you to be an irregular giver to God and His work.

7:3 Melchizedek was compared to Jesus in His priesthood. Melchizedek had no beginning and no end, just like Jesus. He appeared on the scene "suddenly" and then he was gone, which makes him a "type" or "shadow" of Jesus in the Old Testament. A type is something that represents some aspect of the ultimate reality, as a shadow represents the general outline or substance of the object creating it. Melchizedek was a type of Jesus' High Priestly ministry.

> [4] Just think how great he was: Even the patriarch Abraham gave him a tenth of the plunder! [5] Now the law requires the descendants of Levi who become priests to collect a tenth from the people-that is, their brothers-even though their brothers are descended from Abraham. [6] This man, however, did not trace his descent from Levi, yet he collected a tenth from Abraham and blessed him who had the promises. [7] And without doubt the lesser person is blessed by the greater. [8] In the one case, the tenth is collected by men who die; but in the other case, by him who is declared to be living. [9] One might even say

> that Levi, who collects the tenth, paid the tenth through Abraham, [10]because when Melchizedek met Abraham, Levi was still in the body of his ancestor.

7:4 Abraham recognized Melchizedek and honored him with a tithe. I give not because of my faith in giving, but my recognition of my High Priest, Jesus. I give because of who He is, not what He can do for me. If you don't believe in the tithe, I support that perspective, but *only* if you are a generous and regular giver without the guideline of a tithe.

7:5-10 Remember that the writer was addressing a Jewish audience. The writer made a case that Jesus was a High Priest like Melchizedek. Since Abraham responded to Melchizedek with a tithe, then Abraham the lesser was responding to someone greater. In a way, Abraham was recognizing the superiority of Jesus' High Priesthood over against the priesthood of Levi, Abraham's great grandson.

The message was clear: for a believing Jew to return to Judaism once having been a Christian was a step backward, not forward. It would be a return to an inferior system with an inferior priesthood. Abraham, representing the whole world of Old Testament worship, showed his reverence for the new system to come in Christ when he honored Melchizedek with a tithe.

Jesus reigns supreme. There is no one like Him. The writer was smashing any romantic ideas of how the predictable Old Testament system of worship and sacrifice could be superior to anything in the New Testament. That wasn't possible. Then he goes back before to the Law to give an example of how the Law was only a tutor to lead us, Jews and Gentiles, to Jesus.

It's all about Jesus, isn't it? We have made it complicated at times, but it's all about exalting and serving Him. No system, denomination, doctrine, or movement can supersede or overshadow His majesty. There is no alternative to worshiping Him with a whole heart.

I have been guilty of teaching many things other than Jesus. I have exalted myself, other men, and the seeming wisdom of my "insights" over and above Jesus. I preached whole sermons where I didn't even mention His name. These studies, however, have helped me see the reality and focus of the New Testament and those are Jesus, pure and simple. He is the reality of the Old Testament as well.

I want to exalt Jesus, talk about Jesus, teach people to trust in Jesus, and direct people to Him for their every need. There were also times when I tried to take the place of Jesus, trying to be for someone else what only He can be. *Lord, forgive me for my weakness and failure. Help me to exalt You in work, speech, and lifestyle. Amen.*

Have you strayed from a purity and simplicity of focus on Jesus? Do you see Him as a way or *the* Way? The writer of Hebrews saw Him as the latter; you would do well to do the same.

> ¹¹If perfection could have been attained through the Levitical priesthood (for on the basis of it the law was given to the people), why was there still need for another priest to come-one in the order of Melchizedek, not in the order of Aaron? ¹²For when there is a change of the priesthood, there must also be a change of the law. ¹³He of whom these things are said belonged to a different tribe, and no one

from that tribe has ever served at the altar. ¹⁴For it is clear that our Lord descended from Judah, and in regard to that tribe Moses said nothing about priests.

7:11-14 Whoever wrote this letter—and it is my belief that Paul at least collaborated with someone to produce this masterpiece—was thoroughly familiar with Judaism. This was a believing Jew writing to wavering Jews who also believed. Only a Jew could have understood this change of priesthood, but they could have only seen this under the inspiration of the Holy Spirit. This insight is "divine" material indeed. Peter wrote,

> We did not follow cleverly invented stories when we told you about the power and coming of our Lord Jesus Christ, but we were eyewitnesses of his majesty. For he received honor and glory from God the Father when the voice came to him from the Majestic Glory, saying, "This is my Son, whom I love; with him I am well pleased." We ourselves heard this voice that came from heaven when we were with him on the sacred mountain. And we have the word of the prophets made more certain, and you will do well to pay attention to it, as to a light shining in a dark place, until the day dawns and the morning star rises in your hearts. Above all, you must understand that no prophecy of Scripture came about by the prophet's own interpretation. For prophecy never had its origin in the will of man, but men spoke from God as they were carried along by the Holy Spirit (2 Peter 1:16-21).

Peter indicated that the disciples actually heard God's voice from heaven when they were with Jesus (see

Matthew 17:5-6). The word of God, however, is more certain and reliable than the voice Peter and the disciples heard at the Transfiguration. When men around heard the voice of God to which Peter was referring, some thought it was thunder and others thought it was an angel (see John 12:28). A voice from heaven can be misinterpreted, which is why the word of God is so important in the life of every believer. It is a solid rock upon which we place our trust. We can easily mis-hear a voice from heaven, but if we submit to its authority, the written Word can lead and guide us with certainty.

People often say if they would or could hear the voice of God, then they would know and do God's will. That may or may not be true, for we can hear His voice but because of our thinking, we may miss what He is saying. For example, you may be with someone at a party or another social setting and they are talking. They then say your name and because you did not know they were talking to you, you missed everything they said. You heard their voice, but you did not understand what they said.

That is possible even when you read the Word. The Word says to be generous and give, but your thinking is, "God says through His word to give to the poor, but I am poor, so the Word cannot be saying to me to give." The Word says go into all the world, but your thinking is, "I am too old, too young, my health is not good, I don't travel well, so the Word cannot be speaking to me." **Are you not grasping what God is saying to you because you don't believe He is talking to you?** Don't answer too quickly, but ask Him to show you if you are.

The writer went on to explain why Jesus needed to be from the non-priestly tribe of Judah. God was doing a new thing and this new thing required a new priesthood. Jesus could not follow the lineage of Aaron for His priesthood, because His priesthood ushered in a new era in God's relationship with mankind.

So what does this have to do with us? First, we rejoice that our High Priest is Jesus. That means we are free from the Law and under grace. Second, we are free from the futility of a system that required endless sacrifices and empty ritual. Finally, our High Priest is alive, well, and living at the right hand of the Father, interceding for us. This was a difficult adjustment for first-century Jews, but their ambivalence is our certainty. Jesus is my High Priest and He is yours, too. Don't settle for anything or anyone of lesser importance. Let Him represent you on high where the Father lives and take full advantage of His heavenly "connections."

> [15] And what we have said is even more clear if another priest like Melchizedek appears, [16] one who has become a priest not on the basis of a regulation as to his ancestry but on the basis of the power of an indestructible life. [17] For it is declared: "You are a priest forever, in the order of Melchizedek." [18] The former regulation is set aside because it was weak and useless [19] (for the law made nothing perfect), and a better hope is introduced, by which we draw near to God.

7:15-16 At this point, I have completed studies of every New Testament book. In my studies, I have noticed that Paul spent considerable time in Galatians and Romans addressing the issue of the Law and grace, trying to convince the readers that Jesus represented a better way than the Law and Temple regulations ever provided. Here the writer addressed the same issue.

Paul wrote his letters to the Galatians, Romans, and Corinthians to combat the attacks on the gospel he preached to the Gentiles, for self-appointed Jewish believers followed Paul's itinerary and taught that Paul was a false apostle who was teaching a perverted gospel. These Judaizers, as they are called today, claimed that Gentile believers could come to Christ in faith but then had to follow the Law, and that meant the males had to be circumcised. Paul vehemently opposed those teachers, and from his opposition and defense came his clear declaration of justification by faith and faith alone.

This is what feeds my theory that Paul had a hand in writing Hebrews. We know that he loved his Jewish people and would have traded places with them so they could know the truth as he did. He would have had a pastor's heart to see those who did believe in Christ not return to Judaism, which was the appeal of this letter. If Paul had written the letter anonymously, his style and themes could have been recognized and rejected, for many believing Jews did not care for Paul and his ministry:

> Then they said to Paul: "You see, brother, how many thousands of Jews have believed, and all of them are zealous for the law. They have been informed that you teach all the Jews who live among the Gentiles to turn away from Moses, telling them not to circumcise their children or live according to our customs. What shall we do? They will certainly hear that you have come, so do what we tell you. There are four men with us who have made a vow. Take these men, join in their purification rites and pay their expenses, so that they can have their heads shaved. Then everyone will know there is no truth in these reports about

you, but that you yourself are living in obedience to the law. As for the Gentile believers, we have written to them our decision that they should abstain from food sacrificed to idols, from blood, from the meat of strangled animals and from sexual immorality" (Acts 21:20-25).

The apostles had approved Paul's message, but they were still in Jerusalem where the believing Jews visited the Temple and maintained a kosher lifestyle. Their advice to Paul was naïve and designed to win over Jews who could never be won over. In the next chapter of Acts, they seized Paul while he was carrying out the apostles' plan and would have torn him apart had not the Roman guards intervened. That is how much they hated Paul, or at least hated what he represented.

The issue of legalism is still prevalent in the Church today, making the issue of the Law as important today as it was 2,000 years ago. We are all fundamentally religious, created to worship and searching for some system that will codify and structure service to and relationship with God. The Lord isn't interested in a system, but a relationship with His people. If the early writers spent a lot of time addressing legalism, then perhaps we should too.

We want a system because we want God to be predictable so we can control Him. Whenever that happens, we become God because we have found principles that can force Him to do what we want Him to do. God will not permit that to happen.

The writer stated that Jesus' priesthood was based not on the past but the present and future. His priesthood wasn't based on the family tree but eternal life. By that I mean that Jesus did not come to teach men to follow the Law, but to give them eternal life, something which He possessed and had the power to bestow.

7:17 Jesus can perform His priestly duties forever because He lives forever. There is no end to His priesthood, as there was to every Levitical priest. They all died, but Jesus keeps ministering, because He has no end, just like Melchizedek.

7:18-19 The former regulation for the priesthood and the Law was put aside in Christ. We now draw near to God through a better hope by far—the hope of Jesus and His eternal priesthood. Yet the readers were considering whether to abandon this hope for the reliability and predictability of the Old Testament Law. **On what basis do you draw near to God? On weak regulations and legalism or strong and eternal hope in the Son of God who lives forever?** The answer is important, for it will determine how you relate to God and His promises.

> [20] And it was not without an oath! Others became priests without any oath, [21] but he became a priest with an oath when God said to him: "The Lord has sworn and will not change his mind: 'You are a priest forever.'" [22] Because of this oath, Jesus has become the guarantee of a better covenant. [23] Now there have been many of those priests, since death prevented them from continuing in office; [24] but because Jesus lives forever, he has a permanent priesthood. [25] Therefore he is able to save completely those who come to God through him, because he always lives to intercede for them.

7:20-22 God swore an oath that Jesus will be a priest forever. There is not a "new thing" that will come along to change that fact. We can count on Jesus fulfilling His promise to save us because He will live forever according to that promise and because of the reliability of His sinless life—He cannot lie.

One of the themes in Hebrews is the use of the word "better." The writer was pointing out to the believing Jews that what they had under Jesus was better than what they had under the Law. The same is true for you and me. A relationship with Jesus is better than trying to follow rules and guidelines to earn God's favor. Yet the temptation to submit to rules after we know Jesus is still strong. We take on a mentality that we "have" to do things, instead of seeing that we "get" the privilege of serving God.

We have a better covenant—a contract or agreement with God—than the Old Testament could ever offer. Yet some still trade it away for a lesser deal, one that cannot bring life or fulfillment. Others have a romantic attachment to certain rituals, feeling those rituals provide some kind of relationship with God. **Have you done this? Are you living in the fullness of this better covenant or in the seeming comfort and reliability of customs that give the appearance of spirituality but are empty religious practices?**

God is a covenant-making and covenant-keeping God. He only relates to mankind through the use of covenants—always has and always will. He made covenants with Adam, Noah, and David in the Old Testament, and now He relates to those in Christ through the New Covenant established in the blood of Jesus. The older covenants were done away in Christ, so to try and relate to God on the basis of an old covenant is futile, for they have been abolished, and are far inferior to the one established with and through the blood of the Lamb.

Then He took the cup, and gave thanks, and gave *it* to them, saying, "Drink from it, all of you. For this is My blood of the *new covenant*, which is shed for many for the remission of sins. But I say to you, I will not drink of this fruit of the vine from now on until that day when I drink it new with you in My Father's kingdom" (Matthew 26:27-29 NKJV, emphasis added).

Jesus thought and taught in terms of covenant and before He departed made sure He did what He had come to do: establish a new covenant.

7:23-25 Heaven or the next age is comprised of more than one eternal song service. We will have purpose in the next age as we do in this one, but we will be able to carry out our purpose without the limitation of fatigue, hunger, or limited knowledge. Why do I say this here?

I mention that because Jesus went to sit at the right hand of the Father; He went with purpose. He went not to sit and have angels adore and worship Him, but to intercede for those whom He has saved. Jesus is working in heaven and you will, too. What's more, Jesus is working in heaven with the glorified flesh of His resurrection. Did it ever occur to you that when Jesus came back from the dead, He bore the scars in His body of His "previous life?" He also had perfect memory of what had happened to Him before He died. Jesus carried with Him into His new state the remnant and consciousness of His previous state. Here is one author's attempt to explain what the heavenly age will be like. If he is accurate, then what we do now will be important to what we will do later:

> It is work [in heaven] as free from care and toil and fatigue as is the wing-stroke of the jubilant lark when it soars into the sunlight of a fresh, clear day and, spontaneously and for

self-relief, pours out it thrilling carol. Work up there [heaven] is a matter of self-relief, as well as a matter of obedience to the ruling will of God. It is work according to one's tastes and delight and ability. If tastes vary there, if abilities vary there, then occupations vary there (*The Biblical Doctrine of Heaven* by Wilbur M. Smith, Moody Press, 1976, page 192).

That's important to remember because what we do now, learn now, and perfect now will probably be with us for all eternity. What we do today prepares us for what we will do in the future. Jesus is still a priest because He will live forever. What we are, we will be forever because we have eternal life through our relationship with Him.

What can you do today to prepare yourself for eternity? It's a sobering and exciting question, don't you think?

> ²⁶Such a high priest meets our need-one who is holy, blameless, pure, set apart from sinners, exalted above the heavens. ²⁷Unlike the other high priests, he does not need to offer sacrifices day after day, first for his own sins, and then for the sins of the people. He sacrificed for their sins once for all when he offered himself. ²⁸For the law appoints as high priests men who are weak; but the oath, which came after the law, appointed the Son, who has been made perfect forever.

7:26-28 Christ is the focus of the Bible, both Old and New Testaments. He is the central figure and theme. Hebrews reiterated this truth and was written to reinforce this indisputable fact in the minds of the believing Jews to whom it was addressed.

Jesus was and is perfect. He didn't need to make atonement for His own sins before He atoned for the sins of others. His was an efficient and perfect priesthood to serve the needs of men. And He is the Son of God, so His sacrifice was perfect. Everything that needed to be done for man's salvation has already been done. Man cannot supplement this already perfect redemption. Jews needed to be reminded that the ultimate sacrifice had been made and that no other sacrifice could have the effect or meaning of Christ on the cross. **How could they think of turning back to what was inferior when they had the best?** That is question that the writer was posing to the readers.

Yet people alway try to circumvent the importance and necessity of Christ, coming up with new teachings and movements that contain something unique. I am not saying we shouldn't grow in our understanding of God—what He wants and who He is. If any movement doesn't have Jesus as the central focus, however, then it is counterproductive and incomplete, as important or profound as that movement makes itself out to be.

Are you growing in your devotion to Jesus? Do you love Him more this year than last? Are you growing in your knowledge of Him, appreciating every facet of His perfection, love, and work? Read what Paul wrote to the Colossians and see if you can identify the objectives that God has for your life in Christ:

> For this reason, since the day we heard about you, we have not stopped praying for you and asking **God to fill you with the knowledge of his will** through all spiritual wisdom and understanding. And we pray this in order that you may **live a life worthy of the Lord** and may **please him in every**

way: **bearing fruit in every good work, growing in the knowledge of God, being strengthened with all power according to his glorious might** so that **you may have great endurance and patience,** and **joyfully giving thanks to the Father**, who has qualified you to share in the inheritance of the saints in the kingdom of light. For he has rescued us from the dominion of darkness and brought us into the kingdom of the Son he loves, in whom we have redemption, the forgiveness of sins. He is the image of the invisible God, the firstborn over all creation. For by him all things were created: things in heaven and on earth, visible and invisible, whether thrones or powers or rulers or authorities; all things were created by him and for him. He is before all things, and in him all things hold together. And he is the head of the body, the church; he is the beginning and the firstborn from among the dead, so that in everything he might have the supremacy. For God was pleased to have all his fullness dwell in him, and through him to **reconcile to himself all things,** whether things on earth or things in heaven, **by making peace through his blood**, shed on the cross (Colossians 1:9-20, emphasis added).

So how many objectives did you identify? Go back and see what I have highlighted in bold and see how many you found.

8

The point of what we are saying is this: We do have such a high priest, who sat down at the right hand of the throne of the Majesty in heaven, ²and who serves in the sanctuary, the true tabernacle set up by the Lord, not by man. ³Every high priest is appointed to offer both gifts and sacrifices, and so it was necessary for this one also to have something to offer. ⁴If he were on earth, he would not be a priest, for there are already men who offer the gifts prescribed by the law. ⁵They serve at a sanctuary that is a copy and shadow of what is in heaven. This is why Moses was warned when he was about to build the tabernacle: "See to it that you make everything according to the pattern shown you on the mountain."

8:1-2 The things of the Old Testament—the sacrifices, holy days, festivals, and regulations—were types or shadows of heavenly realities. The wilderness tabernacle was a type of worship—giving a pattern for how to proceed into God's presence. The tabernacle furnishings were types of Christ. The golden lampstand, for example, was a type of the only light that is to be present in the believer's life and worship—the life and light of Jesus. The old covenant priests were only shadows of the priest who was to come, namely Jesus. It is beneficial to study the Old Testament from this perspective and see the spiritual reality behind the earthly manifestation. **Why not choose one Old Testament character, or one sacrifice, or one festival and see what of Jesus is reflected in those Old Testament types?**

8:3-4 Jesus' priestly environment wasn't earth, for there were already priests here doing what priests were assigned to do. Instead, Jesus was a heavenly priest and He presides over the heavenly realities of the things of God rather than their earthly shadows. But a heavenly priest would have to be much better than the earthly priests because of the heavenly perfection being served. Remember, the theme of Hebrews is that Jesus provides a "better everything" when compared with Judaism or any legalistic aspect of the Jewish system.

Perhaps you need to stop here and simply worship the Lord for His goodness to you. In Jesus, God has provided everything you need for godliness and righteousness. Let's worship the Lord together for His goodness and celebrate the magnificence and superiority of Christ to all other gods or systems.

8:5 When you read the accounts of the tabernacle construction in Exodus, it is tempting to skip over them because they are repetitious. The Lord was instilling an attitude of precision in the Israelites, however, when it came to the things of God and that is why He went into so much detail. They were never to make the tabernacle or Temple the romantic focus of their worship; those two entities were only a training ground to teach them about a holy God.

Remember that the Lord took a people from Egypt who had little awareness of who He was and built them slowly into His people. That is why there is so much attention given to the details of the tabernacle and Temple. Today that specificity belongs to the mission and person of Jesus. No one is permitted to make Him a creation of their own desire and imagination. He is the fullness and likeness of God, so it is critical that we fashion our image of God according to the truth of who He is, not who we want Him to be:

> So the law was put in charge to lead us to Christ that we might be justified by faith. Now that faith has come, we are no longer under the supervision of the law (Galatians 3:24-25).

When Christ died, the dietary, civil, and sacrificial statutes died with Him. Perhaps it is better to say that we died to those things, because something better, really someone better, came along. Now we are alive in Christ, He is our priest and those things of the past have value to instruct us, but they have no power over, benefit to, or attraction to us.

> ⁶But the ministry Jesus has received is as superior to theirs as the covenant of which he is mediator is superior to the old one, and it is founded on better promises. ⁷For if there had been nothing wrong with that first covenant, no place would have been sought for another. ⁸But God found fault with the people and said: "The time

is coming, declares the Lord, when I will make a new covenant with the house of Israel and with the house of Judah. ⁹It will not be like the covenant I made with their forefathers when I took them by the hand to lead them out of Egypt, because they did not remain faithful to my covenant, and I turned away from them, declares the Lord. ¹⁰This is the covenant I will make with the house of Israel after that time, declares the Lord. I will put my laws in their minds and write them on their hearts. I will be their God, and they will be my people. ¹¹No longer will a man teach his neighbor, or a man his brother, saying, 'Know the Lord,' because they will all know me, from the least of them to the greatest. ¹²For I will forgive their wickedness and will remember their sins no more." ¹³By calling this covenant "new," he has made the first one obsolete; and what is obsolete and aging will soon disappear.

8:6 Once again we see the word "better." We have a superior covenant because Jesus instituted and maintains that covenant. Jesus is better than the system of the Law, but He is also better than Islam, Buddhism, and Hinduism. He is superior to any religious system because He is alive and able to oversee and administer His promises, which include forgiveness of sins and eternal life.

8:7-8 Israel was warned and instructed that a new covenant was coming to replace the old, but they could not surrender the familiarity of the old to the new. Even after some came into this new covenant, they were considering returning to the old. This is remarkable but true, and the same happens today. Some who began well falter as their expectations of what God would and would not do are not met. They then settle for a form of religion that lacks the dynamic relationship with Christ they once had as we read happened in the Ephesians church:

> "Yet I hold this against you: You have forsaken the love you had at first. Consider how far you have fallen! Repent and do the things you did at first. If you do not repent, I will come to you and remove your lampstand from its place" (Revelation 2:4-5).

What about you? Have you settled for a form of religion? Have you abandoned the love and zeal you had when you first met Christ? Are you disappointed with your walk with Christ or His church? Have you lost the zeal you once had?

8:9-10 Looking back, God made it clear that what He was going to do was what the writer had promised God would do in Jeremiah 31:31-34:

> "The days are coming," declares the Lord, "when I will make a new covenant with the people of Israel and with the people of Judah. [32] It will not be like the covenant I made with their ancestors when I took them by the hand to lead them out of Egypt, because they broke my covenant, though I was a husband to them," declares the Lord. "This is the covenant I will make with the people of Israel after that time," declares the Lord. "I will put my law in their minds and write it on their hearts. I will be their God, and they will be my people. No longer will they teach their neighbor, or say to one another, 'Know the Lord,'

because they will all know me, from the least of them to the greatest," declares the Lord. "For I will forgive their wickedness and will remember their sins no more."

Furthermore, it is clear that what He promised to do He has done through Christ and the New Covenant. The Old Covenant was a system of externals, but clearly the New Covenant is one of internals. God now lives in us and He has changed us from within. He has written His requirements on our heart and then helps us carry out those requirements.

The old system was meant to teach people that they did not have it in themselves to do the will of God. They were to become wearied by the endless sacrifice and cleansing that was necessary due to their inability to please God. Jesus then was to represent a better way to God. When Jesus came, however, men had become sentimentally attached to the system, while others made money or held power over people's lives through that old system. For these and other reasons, many rejected the new system in favor of the old. The very system God instituted was used to kill God (Jesus). That is truly ironic.

I don't ever want to develop a system that refers to Jesus but actually excludes Him from my life and worship. I want the Lord to write His law in my mind and heart, because my mind and heart are prone to wander. If I'm not careful, I'll write other things on my heart instead of God's laws and ways.

Lord, keep me from being religious. Deliver me from systems that talk about You, but don't truly represent You. Don't let me forsake the superior for the inferior. I thank You for Your covenant with me in the blood of Jesus. I thank You for my High Priest, Jesus Christ. I want to always be numbered among Your people and I want You to be my God. Amen.

8:11-13 The writer continued the quote taken from Jeremiah 31:31-34. It is interesting the promise of the New Covenant was that each person would know the Lord and would have no need for teachers. I am reminded of what John wrote in his epistle:

> I am writing these things to you about those who are trying to lead you astray. As for you, the anointing you received from him remains in you, and you do not need anyone to teach you. But as his anointing teaches you about all things and as that anointing is real, not counterfeit—just as it has taught you, remain in him (1 John 2:26-27).

John stated that we have no need of anyone to teach us. Yet we know that a teacher is listed among the five-fold ministry of the apostle, prophet, evangelist, pastor, and teacher, so John could not have been eliminating the critical role of the teacher. What was he saying?

John was saying and Jeremiah was predicting that the presence of the Spirit in each believer's life would give him or her access to the inner witness of God's truth. We have been taught, for the most part, not to trust what God is doing inside of us because it may be off or wrong. That has deprived the believer of his or her ability to have confidence in God. *I do not put my faith in my ability to hear God; I put my faith in God's ability to communicate with me.* Part of that communication is the inner anointing of the Spirit, who has come to lead and guide us into all truth. I like how Proverbs 16:3 reads in the Amplified Version:

> Roll your works upon the Lord—commit and trust them wholly to him—and he will cause your thoughts to be agreeable to his will, and so shall your plans be established and succeed.

Why do you mistrust what is in you? Why are you

surprised you can have the mind of Christ today? What inner truth do you have, along with the confirmation of the Spirit, which you are not acting on? Stop putting your trust in your ability to *hear*, but rather place your faith in God's ability to *lead*. Then go do what you sense He is saying to you. The former age of legalism is dead; the new age of the Spirit is here—and that Spirit lives in you. Your sins are forgiven; God is guiding you from within. **Isn't it time you put your trust in Him and acted accordingly?**

9

Now the first covenant had regulations for worship and also an earthly sanctuary. ²A tabernacle was set up. In its first room were the lampstand, the table and the consecrated bread; this was called the Holy Place. ³Behind the second curtain was a room called the Most Holy Place, ⁴which had the golden altar of incense and the gold-covered ark of the covenant. This ark contained the gold jar of manna, Aaron's staff that had budded, and the stone tablets of the covenant. ⁵Above the ark were the cherubim of the Glory, overshadowing the atonement cover. But we cannot discuss these things in detail now.

9:1 God was specific about how the Levites were to assemble the tabernacle. **What was the lesson in that?** It was that God prescribed and still prescribes a specific way to come close to Him. The Levites had to come to God on His terms and in a way that pleased Him—a way that He had established. As I mentioned before, this was a type or shadow of things to come in Jesus. For then, the tabernacle was training Israel concerning how to worship God in a way that was pleasing to Him, not to them. Today that specific way to God is no longer a temple or tabernacle, but Jesus Himself.

Worship isn't about us, it's about Him. We don't choose when and how to worship God; that is His choice. I am always amused by someone who says they have given their life to Jesus, but who doesn't want to lift his or her hands. Worship isn't for our comfort or convenience; it's to glorify God and declare His attributes. God establishes the means by which we render worship unto Him.

9:2 The first room in the wilderness tabernacle had the bread and the lampstand in it. **Can you see how these two things represented Jesus? Wasn't Jesus the bread that came down from heaven (see John 6:33)? Isn't Jesus the light of the world (see John 14:6)?** There is no longer a holy place in which we worship the Lord; we are now a holy people and God chooses to tabernacle in our midst. We live our lives through the nourishment of His sacrifice and walk in the light of His word and guidance through the Holy Spirit.

9:3-4 The Most Holy Place was separated from the first room by a curtain; only the High Priest could go behind that curtain and do that only once a year. **Can you see the symbolism here?** There was an altar of incense; prayer is almost always symbolized by incense in the Bible. **What does Jesus do in the Most Holy Place of heaven today?** He is interceding for us. Only He was qualified to go into that Most Holy Place as our High Priest, and He went in to offer a sacrifice and intercede for us.

The Most Holy Place also had the ark, which contained the manna (which came down from heaven daily to feed the Israelites in the desert—symbolic of God's word that comes daily to feed His people); Aaron's staff (symbolic of God's anointing on His servants); and the tablets of the Law (symbolic of God's truth and righteous requirements). **Can you see how all these things represented Jesus in His earthly ministry?**

The ark was covered with gold, symbolic of Jesus' divinity, while the contents in the ark represented His humanity—a perfect combination found in Jesus, who was fully God and fully man, like us in every way except sin.

9:5 The typology and symbolism of the Old Testament are rich and worthy of study. We must never forget, however, that they all direct us to Jesus, who is worthy of greater honor and who should be the object of our meditation. Let us never get so enamored with the symbols that we forget why they were given: to explain, symbolize, and magnify Jesus. The writer had quickly outlined the tabernacle layout, but then moved on. We need to do the same in our studies: study the Old Covenant but then quickly move on to the real object of our attention, affection, and illumination, and that person is Jesus.

> ⁶When everything had been arranged like this, the priests entered regularly into the outer room to carry on their ministry. ⁷But only the high priest entered the inner room, and that only once a year, and never without blood, which he offered for himself and for the sins the people had committed in ignorance. ⁸The Holy Spirit was showing by this that the way into the Most Holy Place had not yet been disclosed as long as the first tabernacle was

still standing. ⁹This is an illustration for the present time, indicating that the gifts and sacrifices being offered were not able to clear the conscience of the worshiper. ¹⁰They are only a matter of food and drink and various ceremonial washings-external regulations applying until the time of the new order. ¹¹When Christ came as high priest of the good things that are already here, he went through the greater and more perfect tabernacle that is not man-made, that is to say, not a part of this creation. ¹²He did not enter by means of the blood of goats and calves; but he entered the Most Holy Place once for all by his own blood, having obtained eternal redemption. ¹³The blood of goats and bulls and the ashes of a heifer sprinkled on those who are ceremonially unclean sanctify them so that they are outwardly clean. ¹⁴How much more, then, will the blood of Christ, who through the eternal Spirit offered himself unblemished to God, cleanse our consciences from acts that lead to death, so that we may serve the living God!

9:6-8 What is one of the main themes of Hebrews? It is that the benefits of the New Covenant greatly outweigh the benefits of the old one; the New Covenant is a better covenant. The writer makes it clear that the Holy Spirit was directing and inspiring the things of the Old Covenant in order to lead the people to an appreciation and understanding of the New Covenant. The writer of Hebrews obviously felt that the Old Testament was the inspired word of God, even though there were now Spirit-led changes in the New Covenant that the writer was also trying to explain.

While all God's word is inspired, it is important to interpret His word correctly and accurately. Wherever possible, we should allow God's word to interpret God's word. Here we read the Word explaining the significance of the tabernacle and role of the high priest. The goal was never for the people to come into God's presence through the tabernacle. The goal was for us to come to God through Jesus, the heavenly "Holy Place." Our spiritual goal or focus is not a place, but a relationship.

Some try to make a church building a "holy place," and use words like sanctuary, tabernacle, and temple. I have never understood this terminology or thinking. I favor a more informal church setting and understanding. The building doesn't make us holy, nor is there anything special about a certain place, except that it is a place where God's people assemble. When the people leave, there is no presence left like in the Old Testament tabernacle or Temple.

Our destination is Jesus and where He is, that is holy ground. I do think that the modern church has lost our sense of reverence for the holy, but I don't think a building can restore that. Only focusing on Jesus in our worship, teaching, and programs can restore that. If we choose to make a building holy, we have developed a convenient substitute for what can only come by holy living and reverent personal and corporate heart worship.

How do you feel about informal church? For example, should people be allowed to bring coffee and something to eat into the auditorium where church is conducted? Why or why not?

9:9-12 The rituals of the Old Testament were instituted to teach Israel about holiness and to accustom them to the fact that God set the standards for how to approach Him. These rituals were actually given to frustrate people and their attempts to approach God. God would then ultimately solve this frustration with Jesus, doing away with the Temple rituals. But a professional class of priests and clergy appeared who made an even more elaborate system and they and the people became emotionally, religiously, and economically attached to this ritualistic, legalistic system.

I have written previously that this old system, instituted to bring people to God by God, was used to kill God when He came to modify the system He had instituted. The Jews preferred God's system to God. That is how religious people can become—so enamored with the things of God that they forget God or think the system can be their god. The writer of Hebrews was trying to convince the readers not to return to this useless, insipid, and ritualistic system, but to remain true to Christ.

I found this quote from Clark Pinnock in his book, *The Scripture Principle*. It is applicable to what the writer of Hebrews was trying to say:

> It is also clear that God engaged Israel in a process of education that was meant to take them from a lower to a higher plane of religion and morality. It is very important in interpreting the Bible to recognize the principle of progressive revelation. God's truth is not given all at once. The light begins dimly and grows brighter. Seeds are planted early that grow into mature trees. Revelation takes human beings where it finds them and does with them what it can. The old covenant was replaced by a new covenant. The

promise was met with fulfillment. Values relating to power and wealth expressed in the Old Testament were sharpened and deepened in the New Testament. Jesus introduced changes in Old Testament Sabbath law, whereas Paul declared circumcision not to be binding upon Christians. In the soil of the Old Testament texts God laid down principles that would flower into a more perfect disclosure of his will (Harper and Row, 1984, page 111).

We must ask ourselves if we have become enamored with the ritual of church instead of the Lord of the Church, Jesus Himself.

9:13-14 The writer stated that first the blood of animals and then the blood of Jesus cleansed our conscience from acts that lead to death so we can serve God. Here are some thoughts about the concept of conscience:

1. It is a real component of every person and is proof to many of the existence of God. **How else could someone have their conscience accuse them of wrongdoing when they haven't even been taught that what they did was wrong?** (see Romans 2:15)?
2. The conscience isn't infallible; it may accuse or defend certain actions falsely.
3. Some have a stronger conscience than others, but the stronger needs to act according to the level of the weaker conscience (see 1 Corinthians 8:10-12).
4. The conscience needs to be educated concerning what is morally right and wrong.
5. The conscience may be correct in its

disposition but should not have the final word as to what action is required (see 1 Corinthians 4:4-5).

I have taught that guilt is often a bad motivator; it sometimes leads you to do an incorrect or inappropriate thing. Don't respond out of guilt; respond to the Spirit's leading in your life and you will always do the proper thing. In other words, if you have a guilty conscience, don't ignore it, but also don't accept it at face value. Paul wrote that his conscience did not bother him about a certain matter, but he did not use that as his source of vindication: "My conscience is clear, but that does not make me innocent. It is the Lord who judges me"(1 Corinthians 4:4).

> [15] For this reason Christ is the mediator of a new covenant, that those who are called may receive the promised eternal inheritance-now that he has died as a ransom to set them free from the sins committed under the first covenant. [16] In the case of a will, it is necessary to prove the death of the one who made it, [17] because a will is in force only when somebody has died; it never takes effect while the one who made it is living. [18] This is why even the first covenant was not put into effect without blood. [19] When Moses had proclaimed every commandment of the law to all the people, he took the blood of calves, together with water, scarlet wool and branches of hyssop, and sprinkled the scroll and all the people. [20] He said, "This is the blood of the covenant, which God has commanded you to keep."

9:15-16 The Old Testament instituted a system requiring endless sacrifice. The New Testament focuses on one sacrifice, namely Christ, and the endless access that those who put their trust in Him have to the benefits of that one sacrifice. I heard someone say once that when we sin, we should run to God and not from Him. That is the power of what Christ did for us.

A guilty conscience can cause us to run from the very source that will cleanse our conscience. Don't allow guilt to ruin or run your life, no matter how badly you've messed up. Run to Jesus and access the forgiveness that is yours.

9:17 The concept of a suffering Messiah was incomprehensible and offensive to Jews, and still is. The writer was trying to help believing Jews overcome the stigma attached to faith in a Savior who was nailed to a tree in a humiliating death. Christ had to die or the New Covenant would not have been put into effect to supersede the Old Covenant. The Jews, however, could not overcome the concept found in Deuteronomy 21:23:

> "You must not leave the body hanging on the pole overnight. Be sure to bury it that same day, because anyone who is hung on a pole is under God's curse. You must not desecrate the land the Lord your God is giving you as an inheritance."

Jesus received the sentence that was due us because of our sins. He became a curse so we would no longer be cursed. Yet the Jews did not understand and still don't:

> Jews demand signs and Greeks look for wisdom, but we preach Christ crucified: a stumbling block to Jews and foolishness to Gentiles, but to those whom God has called, both Jews and Greeks, Christ the power of God and the wisdom of God (1 Corinthians 1:22-24).

It was inconceivable for the writer of Hebrews that believing Jews would return to the Old Testament Law, having once known and tasted of the New Covenant. It is inconceivable today that believers in Christ would somehow romanticize the rituals of the Old Covenant because of their seeming religious piety and meaning. They were all only signposts to what was coming in Christ.

9:18 The "death" concept of sacrifice in the first covenant was there to condition the people to the fact that without death and the shedding of blood, there was no remission of sin. Christ has endured the ultimate death so a new system and way to God could be introduced. Don't let anything take the place of the work of Christ in your life.

9:19-20 Jesus came and established the New Covenant, just like Moses declared the old one. And just like Moses, Jesus shed blood—His own—so that the New Covenant would take effect. The key to understanding the Old Testament is Jesus in the New. Jesus Himself explained this at the Last Supper:

> While they were eating, Jesus took bread, gave thanks and broke it, and gave it to his disciples, saying, "Take and eat; this is my body." Then he took the cup, gave thanks and offered it to them, saying, "Drink from it, all of you. This is my blood of the covenant, which is poured out for many for the forgiveness of sins" (Matthew 26:26-29).

We can see in part why Jesus commanded that this covenant meal be done again and again to commemorate what He had done. Here in Hebrews we read that some were ready to abandon His sacrifice and pursue the memory of an inferior, outdated Temple ritual. We are to celebrate the

New Covenant meal in communion to keep its supremacy uppermost in our minds and hearts.

Maybe today you should celebrate the Lord's Supper with family or friends? It's always good to remember what Jesus did for us, lest we forget or look for some inadequate ritual to do for us what only Jesus has done and can do.

> [21] In the same way, he sprinkled with the blood both the tabernacle and everything used in its ceremonies. [22] In fact, the law requires that nearly everything be cleansed with blood, and without the shedding of blood there is no forgiveness. [23] It was necessary, then, for the copies of the heavenly things to be purified with these sacrifices, but the heavenly things themselves with better sacrifices than these. [24] For Christ did not enter a man-made sanctuary that was only a copy of the true one; he entered heaven itself, now to appear for us in God's presence. [25] Nor did he enter heaven to offer himself again and again, the way the high priest enters the Most Holy Place every year with blood that is not his own. [26] Then Christ would have had to suffer many times since the creation of the world. But now he has appeared once for all at the end of the ages to do away with sin by the sacrifice of himself. [27] Just as man is destined to die once, and after that to face judgment, [28] so Christ was sacrificed once to take away the sins of many people; and he will appear a second

time, not to bear sin, but to bring salvation to those who are waiting for him.

9:21-24 The Old Testament shows that forgiveness of sins is a messy business. First, there was the bleating of animals being sacrificed, with blood and guts everywhere. Then there was the "messy" business of Jesus' crucifixion, the most hideous death that one person has ever devised against another. The price for our forgiveness has been and still is the shedding of blood, but Jesus shed His once and for all. Now anyone and everyone who wants to have access to the power in that blood can do so through faith.

Allow me to share a Bible story about the blood that Moses used to cleanse Aaron and his sons, because it has lessons for us today:

> He then presented the other ram, the ram for the ordination, and Aaron and his sons laid their hands on its head. Moses slaughtered the ram and took some of its blood and put it on the lobe of Aaron's right ear, on the thumb of his right hand and on the big toe of his right foot. Moses also brought Aaron's sons forward and put some of the blood on the lobes of their right ears, on the thumbs of their right hands and on the big toes of their right feet.

> Then he sprinkled blood against the altar on all sides. He took the fat, the fat tail, all the fat around the inner parts, the covering of the liver, both kidneys and their fat and the right thigh. Then from the basket of bread made without yeast, which was before the Lord, he took a cake of bread, and one made with oil, and a wafer; he put these on the fat portions and on the right thigh.

He put all these in the hands of Aaron and his sons and waved them before the Lord as a wave offering. Then Moses took them from their hands and burned them on the altar on top of the burnt offering as an ordination offering, a pleasing aroma, an offering made to the Lord by fire. He also took the breast—Moses' share of the ordination ram—and waved it before the Lord as a wave offering, as the Lord commanded Moses.

Then Moses took some of the anointing oil and some of the blood from the altar and sprinkled them on Aaron and his garments and on his sons and their garments. So he consecrated Aaron and his garments and his sons and their garments (Leviticus 8:22-30).

Aaron and his sons had their ears, thumbs, and big toes anointed with blood. Wherever we go, whatever we do, and whatever we hear must be in the power of the blood of Jesus. Without His death, we cannot hear, act, or go in a way that will please God. We need the mark of Jesus in everything we do—Jesus just isn't some insurance policy against death to gain eternal life. He is to go with us everywhere we go and everything we do should have His mark, the sign of His shed blood, on it.

Then Aaron's beautiful priestly garments were sprinkled with blood. That would be like a sprinkling of blood on a bride's beautiful white wedding dress. That blood would be the first thing anyone would see and some would consider it a terrible waste, a stain that could not be removed. My righteous garments, my outer works and actions, however, are to have that same blood mark—the mark of my Lord, who gave His life for me.

Brothers and sisters, it's all about Jesus. Jesus isn't to

be a side interest in our lives. He is everything. His mark should be on all we do. Jesus paid a high price for us to do the righteous deeds of God, and may we never tire of wearing the blood stains on our being. Jesus died for us and that truth should be evident in all we do. We are sons and daughters of blood and it is a privilege indeed to be so named.

9:25-26 Here were the choices for the people of Jesus' day. They could either subscribe to a system of regular animal sacrifices, which could never really give them a sense of cleansing from sin, or they could put their trust in Jesus and His once-and-for-all sacrifice of Himself, which would give them an eternal reward and knowledge that their sins had been forgiven. It is difficult to imagine that some chose the former, but they did. And some, having chosen Jesus, were considering going back to the sacrificial system.

Yet the temptation is there for anyone to face the option of turning back. When I first met the Lord, I had the expectation, as silly as it sounds, that I would never have car trouble again because I had the Lord in my life. The first time my car broke down was a tough time for me because it confounded my unrealistic expectations. I have talked to many people who have similar unrealistic expectations about what it means to follow the Lord, about what may or may not happen when anyone follows Jesus. Jesus Himself addressed this when He said, "And blessed is he, whosoever shall not be offended in me" (Matthew 11:6).

When Jesus said that His followers would have to eat His flesh and drink His blood, the results were surprising:

> On hearing it, many of his disciples said, "This is a hard teaching. Who can accept it?" Aware that his disciples were grumbling about this,

Jesus said to them, "Does this offend you? What if you see the Son of Man ascend to where he was before! The Spirit gives life; the flesh counts for nothing. The words I have spoken to you are spirit and they are life. Yet there are some of you who do not believe." For Jesus had known from the beginning which of them did not believe and who would betray him. He went on to say, "This is why I told you that no one can come to me unless the Father has enabled him." From this time many of his disciples turned back and no longer followed him (John 6:60-66).

9:27-28 Some Buddhists and Hindus—and many other with no religious allegiance or affiliation—believe in reincarnation. Others believe in karma, which is any action now that can determine someone's future. In other words, the quality of someone's current and future life is determined by that person's behavior in this or in previous lives. This one verse directly addresses both errors. We all get one life and then there is judgment. Karma states that people get a do-over and can be brought back in another form, to be punished for or to enjoy their past sins or good deeds.

Do you believe in either of those concepts? If to, please search the Scriptures and see that neither are taught, endorsed, or present in any of God's word.

10

The law is only a shadow of the good things that are coming-not the realities themselves. For this reason it can never, by the same sacrifices repeated endlessly year after year, make perfect those who draw near to worship. ²If it could, would they not have stopped being offered? For the worshipers would have been cleansed once for all, and would no longer have felt guilty for their sins. ³But those sacrifices are an annual reminder of sins, ⁴because it is impossible for the blood of bulls and goats to take away sins.

10:1 In the verse the word *shadow* or *type* was used again. The Old Testament Law was not the reality or final installment in God's ongoing revelation, but only a shadow, a general outline, of the things to come in Christ. This is a good reminder to make sure that you are worshiping Jesus and not things that talk about Jesus, like your doctrine, beliefs, or preferred translation of the Bible.

10:2 The Old Testament system was a futile system, and it was intended to be just that. There was nothing romantic or religious about it, as some want to portray it today. It was dirty business, with the smell of animals, living and dead, filling the air around the altar. It is hard to imagine anyone settling for that system when they could have Jesus. It is also difficult to imagine anyone settling for *any* system that doesn't have Jesus as its central focus. People do settle for an inferior religious system, however, all the time. Make sure you are not among them.

The Old Testament system required repeated sacrifices. The Law subjected the people to this futility to lead them to the supremacy and superiority of Christ. Unfortunately, the people got emotionally attached to the wrong system and had difficulty breaking free to embrace the once-and-for-all sacrifice of the Lamb of God:

> Before the coming of this faith, we were held in custody under the law, locked up until the faith that was to come would be revealed. So the law was our guardian until Christ came that we might be justified by faith. Now that this faith has come, we are no longer under a guardian. So in Christ Jesus you are all children of God through faith, for all of you who were baptized into Christ have clothed yourselves with Christ. There is neither Jew nor Gentile, neither slave nor free, nor is there male and female, for you are all one in Christ Jesus. If you belong to Christ, then you are Abraham's seed, and heirs according to the promise (Galatians 3:22-29).

10:3-4 The blood of goats and bulls was and is not capable of taking away sins. They were simply a system to instill in us the awareness that without the shedding of blood there is no forgiveness or remission for sin. The bulls and lambs were simply pointing the way to Jesus, but some wanted that animal system to be perpetuated, and others missed it in a nostalgic kind of way.

Jesus died to grant us forgiveness of sins. Jesus Himself declared that He came to forgive sins; if Jesus has forgiven us, we are forgiven indeed: "But that you may know that the Son of Man has authority on earth to forgive sins . . . ." (Mark 2:10).

I hope that you are not still holding your past sins against yourself, because Jesus certainly is not. **If He isn't, why should you? Are you walking in condemnation over sins you have committed? Do you need to ask God to help you be free from the past so you can enjoy His present and future for you *now*?**

> ⁵Therefore, when Christ came into the world, he said: "Sacrifice and offering you did not desire, but a body you prepared for me; ⁶with burnt offerings and sin offerings you were not pleased. ⁷Then I said, 'Here I am—it is written about me in the scroll—I have come to do your will, O God.'" ⁸First he said, "Sacrifices and offerings, burnt offerings and sin offerings you did not desire, nor were you pleased with them" (although the law required them to be made). ⁹Then he said, "Here I am, I have come to do your will." He sets aside the first to establish the second. ¹⁰And by that will, we have been made holy through the sacrifice of the body of Jesus Christ once for all.

10:5-7

The writer quoted from one of the psalms in this passage:

> Sacrifice and offering you did not desire, but my ears you have pierced; burnt offerings and sin offerings you did not require. Then I said, "Here I am, I have come—it is written about me in the scroll. I desire to do your will, O my God; your law is within my heart" (Psalm 40:6-8).

It is of note that the writer left out one portion of the verse, which states, "but my ears you have pierced." The literal word for pierced here is "bore" or "dug out." God didn't desire a lot of animal sacrifices. Instead He wanted a people who would listen to Him and then do His will:

> You do not delight in sacrifice, or I would bring it; you do not take pleasure in burnt offerings. The sacrifices of God are a broken spirit; a broken and contrite heart, O God, you will not despise (Psalm 51:16-17).

We need God's help in order to hear Him. He needs to do a work in our lives and hearts or else we will continue to do what we *think* He wants us to do instead of what He is directing us to do. Consider the following Messianic passage from Isaiah:

> "The Sovereign Lord has given me an instructed tongue, to know the word that sustains the weary. He wakens me morning by morning, wakens my ear to listen like one being taught. The Sovereign Lord has opened my ears, and I have not been rebellious; I have not drawn back. I offered my back to those who beat me, my cheeks to those who pulled out my beard; I did not hide my face from mocking and spitting" (Isaiah 50:4-6).

Part of the explanation for why Jesus gave His life was

to liberate you and me. Another motivation for the cross was that the Father asked Him to do it: "And being found in appearance as a man, he humbled himself and *became obedient to death*—even death on a cross." (Philippians 2:8, emphasis added). Jesus willingly and voluntarily surrendered Himself in obedience to the will of the Father.

Now He asks that we do the same thing: Listen and do the will of God, whatever it may be and regardless of the cost. We should do His will not because we *have* to do it but rather because we are *privileged* to do it. **Are you happy to serve the Lord, or is it a heavy burden? Do you see that your service is for your benefit, that you are not doing the Lord a favor when you obey?**

10:8 Israel should have been eager to abandon the sacrificial system, but instead they worked to perpetuate it, even sacrificing God's Son so their religious way of life could be maintained—or so they thought. Instead, their entire world would be coming to an end in 70 AD when the Romans sacked Jerusalem and destroyed the Temple. Their futile effort to preserve the system that was only meant to lead them to Christ had to be abandoned when God took matters into His own hands and ended for them what they should have abolished for themselves.

There are still people like that today who prefer to perform all manner of sacrifices and religious acts rather than pick up their cross and follow after Jesus in the power of the Spirit:

> Since you died with Christ to the elemental spiritual forces of this world, why, as though you still belonged to the world, do you submit to its rules: "Do not handle! Do not taste! Do not touch!"? These rules, which have to do with things that are all destined to perish with use, are based

on merely human commands and teachings. Such regulations indeed have an appearance of wisdom, with their self-imposed worship, their false humility and their harsh treatment of the body, but they lack any value in restraining sensual indulgence (Colossians 2:20-23).

Not only did not God not prefer burnt offerings, He was not pleased when they were offered. You are never doing God a favor when you perform some act of obedience and devotion. If you have a dollar in your pocket and you wrestle with giving it away but finally do, that does not represent a sacrifice. It indicates money has a hold on you. When you do finally give it, it is a good thing to do but not a freewill offering or sacrifice.

Do you ever have the attitude that you are doing God a favor when you obey? In what area? Do you see your need to change your attitude?

10:9 This phrase, "Here I am," is an important one. When God speaks, that is what we should say. "Here I am" signifies we are ready to do what God wants *before* we know what it is. We aren't saying, "Yeah?" or "What do You want?" We are indicating we have a ready heart to do whatever it is that we are about to hear. Look at Genesis 22:1, 7, 11; Genesis 31:11; Genesis 46:2; Exodus 3:4; and 1 Samuel 3:4. There you have other examples of those who said, "Here I am!" Now you know what to say when you think God is calling your name with something for you to do.

10:10 You have been made holy—set apart for God—through the sacrifice of Jesus' life. There is nothing additional that needs to be done or can be done to make that more of a reality. You are God's because Jesus died for you. **Why not worship Jesus today because of the wonderful thing He has done for you?**

> [11]Day after day every priest stands and performs his religious duties; again and again he offers the same sacrifices, which can never take away sins. [12]But when this priest had offered for all time one sacrifice for sins, he sat down at the right hand of God. [13]Since that time he waits for his enemies to be made his footstool, [14]because by one sacrifice he has made perfect forever those who are being made holy. [15]The Holy Spirit also testifies to us about this. First he says: [16]"This is the covenant I will make with them after that time, says the Lord. I will put my laws in their hearts, and I will write them on their minds." [17]Then he adds: "Their sins and lawless acts I will remember no more." [18]And where these have been forgiven, there is no longer any sacrifice for sin.

10:11-12 Today Jesus is seated at the right hand of God. Jesus our brother, with a body like ours (except that it is glorified), is seated in heaven. He understands us and is interceding for us at God's right hand. Jesus sat down in heaven because there was no other sacrifice that needed to be made, but that doesn't mean Jesus is idle in heaven. He is still seeking and saving the lost through the Holy Spirit and He is praying for us. Heaven will not be a place where you do nothing. If Jesus is working in heaven, then you will too as we saw earlier in this study.

By the way, **do you know what your purpose in life is?** There is a good chance you will be fulfilling your purpose for all eternity, so it would be good to know what it is.

Also, **do you believe Jesus is the only way to the Father? Or have you bought into the modernist thinking that there are many ways to God?** This is an important question because the tolerance of this age would dictate there are many ways to God. It can seem narrow and rigid that there is only one way, but that is certainly what Scripture indicates.

This truth applies even to Israel, for if they do not resolve who Jesus is and accept Him as such, they can have no access to the Father except through Him.

10:13-14 Jesus has finished His work of redemption. There is nothing else that needs to be done on His part. It is now up to men and women to put their faith in the work Jesus did so they can become holy to God. Jesus' work in that regard is finished.

Jesus is now waiting until all those who oppose His work and role are made His footstool. Jesus will put His feet on those who refused to put their feet on Him, the Rock. That will include all those who preferred a religious system as opposed to faith in Christ. Those people, no matter how innocent they may appear, are enemies of Jesus and the Church. That is why the writer was spending so much time trying to dissuade anyone from abandoning their faith in favor of a sacrificial system. We would do well to heed His warning today.

10:15 The writer of this letter had no problem recognizing that the Holy Spirit speaks to men. In this verse the writer stated, "First he says." The 'he' refers to the Spirit. I cannot quite understand the debate on whether or not the Bible is the inspired, inerrant word of God. While we must acknowledge there are probably some minor errors in the manuscripts handed down to us for millennia, there can be no room for a believer to deny that the Scriptures are the work and word of God. The same God who inspired the Scriptures has preserved the Scriptures in the form we have today.

A book entitled *The Scripture Principle* by Clark Pinnock includes more about the debate that has been going on between those who believe the Bible to be God's word and those who believe it to be a book about God, but a collection of myths and human stories that only amount to interesting reading with interesting moral lessons.

10:16 The writer quoted Jeremiah 31:33-34 in this verse, acknowledging that the Holy Spirit was speaking to Jeremiah. The implication is that the New Covenant was not the idea of men but an institution from God. No one, therefore, could alter it. The New Covenant transitioned from a covenant with external effects and expressions to one that worked on the internals of the heart. The Old Covenant could not change men's hearts; it could only convince them that their heart needed a total makeover in order to serve God and fulfill His righteous requirements.

10:17 Some people agonize over their sins, wondering whether or not they are truly forgiven. Forgiveness of our sins isn't based on anything any human can do (except ask for it); forgiveness is part of the New Covenant and the new promise of God. Forgiveness of our sins is based on God's promise and doesn't depend on the magnitude or quantity of our sins.

We can go to God for forgiveness and He will extend it because of His promise in the New Covenant. **Are you struggling whether or not you are forgiven? Are you concerned that your sins are too grievous for God to forgive** or forget? Well, you can rest today, for God's promise and His covenant to you is that He will remember your sins no more. Ask for forgiveness and leave your sins with Him. If He forgets them, **why can't you? Are you holier or more righteous than God?**

The implications for the Jewish reader should have been clear. To return to the Old Covenant would have meant they were abandoning any hope of having their sins forgiven, for the Law could only make them aware of sin but could not deal with the root cause of sin or its effects. Departing from the New Covenant would have been a step back, a leap off a spiritual cliff to one's certain death. As the writer mentioned earlier, this would have been repudiating the need and efficacy of Christ's sacrifice on the cross, and if that happened, there was no other refuge from the wrath of God.

10:18 Once God has forgotten our sins, we would do well not to mention them to Him again. There is no need to apply the sacrifice of Jesus to your sins any longer; once is enough. Not only was this a more righteous system in Christ than the Law provided, it was a more efficient system. Jesus paid the price once and for all so that our sins could be forgiven.

That was the reason sinful people felt so comfortable being with Jesus when He walked the earth. Since He is the same today as He was then, sinners like us should feel just as comfortable. Remember what John wrote:

> This is the message we have heard from him and declare to you: God is light; in him there is no darkness at all. If we claim to have fellowship with him yet walk in the darkness, we lie and do not live by the truth. But if we walk in the light, as he is in the light, we have fellowship with one

another, and the blood of Jesus, his Son, purifies us from all sin. If we claim to be without sin, we deceive ourselves and the truth is not in us. If we confess our sins, he is faithful and just and will forgive us our sins and purify us from all unrighteousness. If we claim we have not sinned, we make him out to be a liar and his word has no place in our lives (1 John 1:5-10).

> [19] Therefore, brothers, since we have confidence to enter the Most Holy Place by the blood of Jesus, [20] by a new and living way opened for us through the curtain, that is, his body, [21] and since we have a great priest over the house of God, [22] let us draw near to God with a sincere heart in full assurance of faith, having our hearts sprinkled to cleanse us from a guilty conscience and having our bodies washed with pure water. [23] Let us hold unswervingly to the hope we profess, for he who promised is faithful. [2e] And let us consider how we may spur one another on toward love and good deeds. [25] Let us not give up meeting together, as some are in the habit of doing, but let us encourage one another-and all the more as you see the Day approaching.

10:19

I heard a teacher say one time, "When you see a therefore in the Bible, find out what it's there for." Finally, the writer has cut to the chase, so to speak. Having spent a lot of time pointing out that the New Covenant in Jesus is superior to the Old Covenant of the

Law, the writer went on to explain the implications of this truth for the believer in Christ.

One important implication is that we can now have confidence to approach God. Our confidence is in Jesus and His accomplished work on the cross, and not our own works or abilities. I heard another teacher say one time, "When you sin, that's not the time to run *from* God but to run *to* God!" **Are you spending more time running to or from God?**

10:20 Another benefit is that we can now enter "behind the curtain" of the heavenly Holy Place. That is the symbolism behind what happened when Jesus died on the cross:

> And when Jesus had cried out again in a loud voice, he gave up his spirit. At that moment the curtain of the temple was torn in two from top to bottom. The earth shook and the rocks split (Matthew 27:50-52).

The way to God was opened through the bodily sacrifice of Jesus. The curtain has been torn and anyone, not just the high priest, can come to God in the Most Holy Place. **Are you coming to God freely and with regularity? Are you taking full advantage of this invitation to His throne room? When you enter, what are you doing? Asking for significant things or rehashing old sins and reminding God of your unworthiness?**

10:21 Jesus is alive and seated in heaven to oversee and ensure that His sacrifice is effectual forever. He is our high priest. We approach God not on our own merits but relying on what Jesus did for us.

10:22 We can approach God with the assurance of faith, not an assurance that we have made every sacrifice or performed every ritual that enables us to come into His presence. When the priest approached the Holy Place in the Old Covenant, this is what he had to do:

> "This is a requirement of the law that the Lord has commanded: Tell the Israelites to bring you a red heifer without defect or blemish and that has never been under a yoke. Give it to Eleazar the priest; it is to be taken outside the camp and slaughtered in his presence. Then Eleazar the priest is to take some of its blood on his finger and sprinkle it seven times toward the front of the Tent of Meeting.
>
> While he watches, the heifer is to be burned—its hide, flesh, blood and offal. The priest is to take some cedar wood, hyssop and scarlet wool and throw them onto the burning heifer. After that, the priest must wash his clothes and bathe himself with water. He may then come into the camp, but he will be ceremonially unclean till evening. The man who burns it must also wash his clothes and bathe with water, and he too will be unclean till evening.
>
> "A man who is clean shall gather up the ashes of the heifer and put them in a ceremonially clean place outside the camp. They shall be kept by the Israelite community for use in the water of cleansing; it is for purification from sin. The man who gathers up the ashes of the heifer must also wash his clothes, and he too will be unclean till evening. This will be a lasting ordinance both for the Israelites and for the aliens living among them" (Numbers 19:2-10).

Contrast this futile and repetitive ritual with the beauty and simplicity of putting faith in Christ and the sacrifice Jesus made. **How could anyone who knew Jesus consider going back to rituals like the one described above?** In addition, the one above was a type or shadow of Jesus, the red heifer of God who was to come. Jesus replaced this ritual, for no one today performs its rites. **Aren't you glad that you are free from a burdensome ritual that needed to be repeated again and again?** Notice also that the priest had to bathe his body when he approached the holy place:

> He is to put on the sacred linen tunic, with linen undergarments next to his body; he is to tie the linen sash around him and put on the linen turban. These are sacred garments; so he must bathe himself with water before he puts them on (Leviticus 16:4).

The writer may have been alluding to the waters of baptism, which is a once-and-for-all ritual that believers must perform. Even if he wasn't referring to baptism, however, he paints a wonderful picture of the benefits of approaching God on the merits of faith in Jesus. In Christ, God cleanses us inside and out. The Old Testament rituals had no power to cleanse or change the worshiper on the inside at the heart level.

10:23 The writer urged the reader to hold on to the confession of hope "unswervingly." That warning indicates that things and situations will occur, trying to make us swerve to avoid a collision. We are to stay on course, however, and trust the Lord, no matter what happens.

Recently I have faced how shallow my faith is and can be in certain areas of my life. I am not unswerving in my trust. I often allow circumstances to shake my confidence and the Lord is trying to work more faith and trust into my lifestyle. When there is little money in my bank account, my trust swerves. When someone is upset with me or questions what I teach or do, my hope swerves. When I have computer problems that I don't understand how to fix, I get uptight and allow my trust and hope to swerve. This shows I am basically an uptight person but God is working in my life to fix this weakness, for He truly is faithful. I can put my full confidence in Him to complete the work He started in me:

> To him who is able to keep you from stumbling and to present you before his glorious presence without fault and with great joy—to the only God our Savior be glory, majesty, power and authority, through Jesus Christ our Lord, before all ages, now and forevermore! Amen (Jude 24-25).

Where are you at in regards to this issue? How firm is your confidence? Do you approach God will full assurance, even when things aren't going well for you? I hope this study will help you as it is helping me. May God reveal to us today the greatness of His love and faithfulness and then may we learn to rely on that faithfulness in good times and in bad.

10:24 We are in this walk together. I am only partially successful if I maintain my walk with the Lord, but do not maintain it with those around me. Notice here that love and good deeds are linked together. We can only prove our love as we engage in good deeds for one another. And stimulating others to good deeds must be strategic—I must give some thought as to how I can do that—making you more ready and eager to do good deeds for others as you observe what I do. Part of that is by example; part is by doing it for and to you so you can feel the effects of God's love for you through me. Then you will want to do the same for others.

This concept of good deeds must be properly understood. We are expected to do good deeds as a result of our relationship with Christ and not to earn or maintain our relationship with Him. The good works are the proof that our walk with Him is real because love is motivating us and because we function now with a new heart put there and energized by the Spirit.

This truth can be confusing when we read what Jesus said in Matthew 25:31-46 where He discussed the sheep and the goats. The sheep did good deeds while the goats did not. Jesus told the crowd that when the sheep did good deeds for others, they were really doing them to and for Him, and then promised,

> "Then the King will say to those on his right, 'Come, you who are blessed by my Father; take your inheritance, the kingdom prepared for you since the creation of the world. For I was hungry and you gave me something to eat, I was thirsty and you gave me something to drink, I was a stranger and you invited me in, I needed clothes and you clothed me, I was sick and you looked after me, I was in prison and you came to visit me'" (Matthew 25:34-36).

Jesus was not insinuating that God would keep a giant scorecard on which He wrote all the good deeds anyone had done. Then, if they had enough good deeds, they would inherit eternal life. What He was indicating, however, is that those who had a relationship with Him would prove it by the good deeds they did. Those who did no good deeds would prove that they did not know Him and would be assigned their eternal destination.

10:25 I am always amused and intrigued by people who walk with the Lord, but don't go to church anywhere. They tell me, "I can worship the Lord just as well at home on Sunday with my family." That is not the standard to which God has called believers. Jesus gave His life to establish the Church; can we do any less?

I admit that it is often easier to maintain our love for the Lord without the interference of imperfect, inconsiderate people (of which I am one). Jesus called us, however, to walk out our obedience to Him in the context of a church body, as difficult as that may be. We may walk out Christ's love to those outside the church, but we can pick and choose when, with whom, and how we will do that. When we are in a church, however, we don't get to pick and choose. God chooses those opportunities for us. John explained this when he wrote,

> We love because he first loved us. If anyone says, "I love God," yet hates his brother, he is a liar. For anyone who does not love his brother, whom he has seen, cannot love God, whom he has not seen. And he has given us this command: Whoever loves God must also love his brother (1 John 4:19-21).

Our love for God and journey with God will never be all that it can be unless we are learning how to express the love of God to other people, especially believers. **Are you in a local church? Have you been injured or offended by churches or church members in the past?** If you are not in a church at the present time, I suggest you find one and join it, whether it meets all your standards or not. If your needs aren't met there, then make it your aim to meet the needs of others and trust God for your own until a better option comes along.

²⁶If we deliberately keep on sinning after we have received the knowledge of the truth, no sacrifice for sins is left, ²⁷but only a fearful expectation of judgment and of raging fire that will consume the enemies of God. ²⁸Anyone who rejected the law of Moses died without mercy on the testimony of two or three witnesses. ²⁹How much more severely do you think a man deserves to be punished who has trampled the Son of God under foot, who has treated as an unholy thing the blood of the covenant that sanctified him, and who has insulted the Spirit of grace? ³⁰For we know him who said, "It is mine to avenge; I will repay," and again, "The Lord will judge his people." ³¹It is a dreadful thing to fall into the hands of the living God.

10:26-27 This reference was once again directed to those who knew Christ but then willingly walked away from Him in search of a better system or "deal" in serving God. There is no sacrifice for any sin at this point in history except for Jesus. Those who reject Him have no hope of a relationship with the Father. Rejecting Christ would make the one rejecting Him an enemy of God. This verse does not pertain to a believer who willingly sins. A case in point would be Peter, who willingly denied Jesus, but found forgiveness and grace from Jesus. You may respond that anyone in Christ could not *willingly* sin if they were rightly related to God, but Paul wrote:

So I find this law at work: When I want to do good, evil is right there with me. For in my inner being I delight in God's law; but I see another law at work in the members of my body, waging war against the law of my mind and making me a prisoner of the law of sin at work within my members. What a wretched man I am! Who will rescue me from this body of death? Thanks be to God-through Jesus Christ our Lord!

So then, I myself in my mind am a slave to God's law, but in the sinful nature a slave to the law of sin. Therefore, there is now no condemnation for those who are in Christ Jesus, because through Christ Jesus the law of the Spirit of life set me free from the law of sin and death. For what the law was powerless to do in that it was weakened by the sinful nature, God did by sending his own Son in the likeness of sinful man to be a sin offering. And so he condemned sin in sinful man, in order that the righteous requirements of the law might be fully met in us, who do not live according to the sinful nature but according to the Spirit (Romans 7:21-8:4).

There is grace for the sinner who turns to Christ; there is none available for those who refuse Him or who knew Him and turn away from Him. As we have seen in First John, God freely forgives those who sin, admit it, and then turn to Him for forgiveness. That process is incomplete if someone walks away from Christ, for then there is no source for their needed forgiveness.

10:28-29 The writer used strong language in this verse: "trampled the Son of God," and "insulted the Spirit of grace." Someone could think that because God is invisible or because He is long-suffering, He cannot be insulted or grieved. God is a being, however, and can be angered, offended, and insulted. It is important that we not interpret God in terms of our own sinful, human tendencies. If God is angered or offended, it is not because He has any inherent weakness or insecurities.

Remember that this letter to the Hebrews was written to those who were considering a departure from the faith and a return to Judaism. To have done so would have insulted God and rejected His solution to mankind's problem of sin. **I do not want to ever insult God, do you?** If your answer is no, then make Jesus the one and only focal point for your life and walk with God.

10:30-31 The writer quoted Deuteronomy 32:35-36 in these verses. God will judge His people to preserve them from His and their enemies, and anyone who walked with Jesus only to turn back would be judged as an enemy of God. It would indeed be dreadful to meet God as an enemy. The writer has turned from passionate pleading and biblical arguments to strong language to keep those considering a return to Judaism from doing so.

There are some who believe that this standard represents God's harshness, but here's another way to look at it. Let's say that when you jump out a plane and are wearing a parachute, you have a good chance of landing safely. Assume for a moment that you refuse to wear your parachute and still jump. When you hit the ground, it will be bad for you, but let's assume you survive. **Do you have the right at that point to shake your fist in anger at God for being injured? Did not God provide the way out of your condition that was caused by your decision to jump from the plane without a parachute?**

Those who reject Christ and then accuse God of being angry or narrow are doing the same thing as the person who jumps without the chute. They reject the simple answer to their sin dilemma but curse God that He has not provided another answer—the answer they want but not the one God wants and has provided in Christ.

> ^{32}Remember those earlier days after you had received the light, when you stood your ground in a great contest in the face of suffering. ^{33}Sometimes you were publicly exposed to insult and persecution; at other times you stood side by side with those who were so treated. ^{34}You sympathized with those in prison and joyfully accepted the confiscation of your property, because you knew that you yourselves had better and lasting possessions. ^{35}So do not throw away your confidence; it will be richly rewarded.

10:32 The readers of this letter had obviously paid a price for their faith at some point in their walk with the Lord. They were subjected to suffering and intense pressure, yet they obviously stood their ground. Any time we take a stand for Jesus, we will face opposition, sometimes intense persecution and tribulation. Peter and John also wrote about this particular fact of life in Christ. Perhaps you need to remind yourself of this today:

> Dear friends, do not be surprised at the painful trial you are suffering, as though something strange were happening to you. But rejoice that you participate in the sufferings of Christ, so that you may be overjoyed when his glory is revealed.

If you are insulted because of the name of Christ, you are blessed, for the Spirit of glory and of God rests on you. If you suffer, it should not be as a murderer or thief or any other kind of criminal, or even as a meddler.

However, if you suffer as a Christian, do not be ashamed, but praise God that you bear that name. For it is time for judgment to begin with the family of God; and if it begins with us, what will the outcome be for those who do not obey the gospel of God? And, "If it is hard for the righteous to be saved, what will become of the ungodly and the sinner?" So then, those who suffer according to God's will should commit themselves to their faithful Creator and continue to do good (1 Peter 4:12-19).

Do not be surprised, my brothers, if the world hates you. We know that we have passed from death to life, because we love our brothers. Anyone who does not love remains in death (1 John 3:13-15).

10:33 Sometimes the suffering for following Christ is a result of a direct personal attack, and other times it is identifying with others who are under attack. To stand with someone else means you have a close enough relationship to know what they are going through. That requires you to not only be in a church but to be in fellowship and relationship with those who are there with you. **Do you have close relationships with other believers? What can you do to develop those relationships?**

At other times, to stand with others means to identify with them and to help them when you can, or at least not to disassociate yourself from them in their hour of need. For example, you can stand with suffering saints in the Middle East, or some other part of the world without knowing them. **Can you think of ways to 'stand with' those who are suffering persecution? What can you do?** You can pray, contribute to those who minister among those saints, or visit them yourself if the opportunity presents itself.

10:34 My "stuff" often has more of a hold on me than I would like to admit. Years ago, my computer, briefcase, and passport were stolen in a foreign country. I felt violated and at such a loss. Then I remembered a story I had read about Hudson Taylor, the great missionary to China. Once he had entrusted all his possessions to someone who was supposed to take them by boat to his next destination. Unfortunately, he never saw his possessions again. I consoled myself after my own loss by thinking, "If Hudson Taylor could endure the loss of all to take the gospel to China, then I can endure this loss for the sake of the work I am doing in this nation for Christ!"

One sign that your "stuff" has a hold on you is whether or not you can give it away. I mentioned earlier that I took my favorite shirt to Cuba when I ministered there. All of us left our clothes there to help the saints, but I struggled leaving that favorite shirt. After wrestling with that issue for three days, I concluded I had no choice but to leave it, because a small piece of blue cloth had a hold on me. I could not let that happen. **Do any pieces of metal, cloth, or plastic have a hold on you? If so, what are willing to do to break their hold?**

10:35 If the writer cautioned us not to throw our confidence away, then that means we have the capability to throw it away. That means confidence is something under our control, but what confidence was the author referring to? The writer was speaking about our confidence in God's word and the Holy Spirit's work in our lives. It also referred to our confidence that Jesus is the only answer to man's addiction to sin. Finally, it is confidence that what God said He would do in Christ He will do—forgive our sins, give us eternal life, and help us overcome sin and the devil in this life. **How is your confidence level today? Have you maintained it or have you allowed it to be eroded?** If it's weak or you have lost it altogether, make a decision to get it back.

> [36] You need to persevere so that when you have done the will of God, you will receive what he has promised. [37] For in just a very little while, "He who is coming will come and will not delay. [38] But my righteous one will live by faith. And if he shrinks back, I will not be pleased with him." [39] But we are not of those who shrink back and are destroyed, but of those who believe and are saved.

10:36 This verse presents an interesting progression. I want to receive God's promises and *then* I feel like I can persevere. God wants me to persevere in doing His will, however, and only then will I receive His promises. The problem is *then*, for I don't know how long the *then* will require. After more than 40 years of walking with Jesus, however, I have learned that the *then* is almost always longer than I thought it would be or wanted it to be! **Are you in a *then* period? Are you waiting to receive God's promise, doing His will faithfully in the meantime?** If so, then be of good cheer. You are doing what's called "waiting on the Lord." Read the following verses and be encouraged to wait:

No one whose hope is in you will ever be put to shame, but they will be put to shame who are treacherous without excuse (Psalm 25:3).

Yet those who wait for the Lord Will gain new strength; They will mount up with wings like eagles. They will run and not get tired, they will walk and not become weary (Isaiah 40:31 NASB).

"Then you will know that I am the Lord; those who hope in me will not be disappointed" (Isaiah 49:23).

If you are waiting on the Lord, you may be in a hard place, but you are also in a good place. Yet waiting does not necessarily mean inactivity. **What can you do today to help prepare you in this *then* time so you will be ready when the *then* is finished?**

10:37-38

It appears the writer of Hebrews paraphrased Habakkuk 2:2-4 in these verses:

"For the revelation awaits an appointed time; it speaks of the end and will not prove false. Though it linger, wait for it; it will certainly come and will not delay. 'See, he is puffed up; his desires are not upright-but the righteous will live by his faith'"

The fulfillment of God's promises always lingers to teach us to trust in Him and not the circumstances around us. The promises linger to teach us trust and faith. In this context, the opposite of faith is being "puffed up" or proud. There was a lyric to a song I heard that made sense where this truth is concerned. It went, "There's only one thing worse than waiting on God and that's wishing that you did." Amen!

Are you waiting on the Lord for some promise or

fulfillment of a vision He has given you? Don't be discouraged, but encourage yourself in the Lord today and let your trust level rise. God is faithful and He cannot lie.

10:39 The word "shrink back" is the word from which we get the English word "apostate." An apostate refers to someone who abandons the faith after having walked in it. The writer wasn't talking about faith for finance or ministry (although we can apply the principle of faith to those issues), but rather about faith for salvation. Obviously there were some who were considering becoming apostate and it was to those the writer addressed this letter.

11

Now faith is being sure of what we hope for and certain of what we do not see. ²This is what the ancients were commended for. ³By faith we understand that the universe was formed at God's command, so that what is seen was not made out of what was visible. ⁴By faith Abel offered God a better sacrifice than Cain did. By faith he was commended as a righteous man, when God spoke well of his offerings. And by faith he still speaks, even though he is dead. ⁵By faith Enoch was taken from this life, so that he did not experience death; he could not be found, because God had taken him away. For before he was taken, he was commended as one who pleased God. ⁶And without faith it is impossible to please God, because anyone who comes to him must believe that he exists and that he rewards those who earnestly seek him.

11:1 We now begin one of the great chapters in the Bible (yes, I know—they're all great; but some are greater). To begin with, faith is being sure of what we hope for. Keep in mind that the context of the letter is faith in Christ, which indicates we can be sure of our salvation. I never give any thought as to whether or not I am saved. I know I am, even though I am saved by faith.

Is it possible to have that kind of certainty in other areas of life and our walk with God? I think so. God can so clearly show us something in faith that we can base our whole life on the certainty of that which He has showed us. For example, I knew for 16 years that I would preach although I had no opportunities. I was so certain in faith, howeer, that I prepared and visualized myself doing so, based not on the amount of ministry opportunities I had but rather on the promise God gave me. Today I preach all over the world because I had confidence and certainty of what God had spoken to me years ago, and I prepared before I ever realized the fulfillment of God's vision and promise. I was sure of what I could not see.

11:2 God commended men and women of old for their faith and He still commends people of faith today. The rest of this chapter contains some of those commendations of the saints of old. I want God to commend me for my faith one day. I have said I would rather die in faith than live in presumption or "un-faith." **How about you? What are you trusting God for that only He can do? What are you believing the Lord for that unless He comes through, you will look foolish?**

11:3 Every theory of how the world began is just that: a theory. Evolutionists talk with certainty, but they weren't there when the world began. Therefore, they have a theory although they talk like they know. I have faith and I believe what I see around me came from what I cannot see—it came from God's command. This is important because God can still provide for us today through His spoken command, creating something out of nothing. He can create a job for us where there wasn't one previously. He can provide for us through people who have never allowed God to use them. God speaks and the world "listens" and responds.

We are connected to all the resources in the universe through Christ. Our source is not the visible, but the invisible word of God. I put my faith in His ability today. **What, in whom, and where are you putting your faith today?**

11:4 **Is it interesting to you that Adam and Eve are not mentioned in the Hebrews 11 faith accounts?** Perhaps they did nothing of faith that pleased God and are passed over in the faith commendations. Instead, God goes directly to address the story of Cain and Abel.

Cain brought an offering from the earth, which God had cursed. Abel brought an offering from the flock, which spoke of the shedding of blood and foreshadowed the forgiveness of sin. Cain probably did not bring a few tomatoes and cucumbers as his offering. Perhaps he brought a magnificent offering of the produce of the soil. That is why he was so angry when God rejected his offering.

Cain brought something to God on his own terms and was rejected, even though it was probably magnificent and impressive. Abel had faith and his offering was received. In fact, the faith with which he brought this offering is still speaking to us today. Many want to leave their children a legacy. The greatest legacy to leave your children is a legacy of faith and trusting God.

11:5 Enoch's story is found in one verse, Genesis 5:22, but what a story it is. Enoch was one who pleased God and we know from this current chapter that faith had to be his chief means of pleasing his Creator. So completely did Enoch walk in faith that he did not see death.

I'm not sure what all that means and what Enoch did exactly. I know that Enoch had a lot less information and spritual resources than we have. He walked in what he had so completely and perfectly, however, that he brought nothing but pleasure to God his Maker. **If Enoch can please God, what should we be able to do?**

Oh Lord, forgive me for how short I come in fulfilling Your expectations. I walk in so little faith, yet that is the very means by which I can bring pleasure to Your heart. I choose to be obedient to You and ask that receive my faith vows as a pleasing sacrifice to You. Amen.

11:6 It is impossible to please God. There is nothing we have that He needs; nothing we can say that will impress Him; nothing we can build that will move Him. There is only one thing that can please God and that is when we put our hands in His and say, "I trust you." Do that today.

The word translated here as *anyone* means just that: *anyone*. Anyone who comes to God must believe that He exists and rewards those who diligently seek Him. The word *diligently* speaks once again to the need to persevere and endure in seeking, to prove that your faith is real. God hides Himself at times not to punish you but to teach you to trust and have faith in Him. When you continue your pursuit of God in the midst of difficulties, you please Him. What's more, He will ultimately reward you. **Are you discouraged in your faith walk?** Press on, dear friend, and keep your trust in God. Don't be deterred and you will be rewarded—although the reward may take a lot longer than you anticipated.

Faith is the currency with which we make transactions with God. Spend it wisely and, when you do, He fills your pockets with more faith to make even more transactions. Faith is not an event, but rather a lifestyle.

> ⁷By faith Noah, when warned about things not yet seen, in holy fear built an ark to save his family. By his faith he condemned the world and became heir of the righteousness that comes by faith. ⁸By faith Abraham, when called to go to a place he would later receive as his inheritance, obeyed and went, even though he did not know where he was going. ⁹By faith he made his home in the promised land like a stranger in a foreign country; he lived in tents, as did Isaac and Jacob, who were heirs with him of the same promise. ¹⁰For he was looking forward to the city with foundations, whose architect and builder is God. ¹¹By faith Abraham, even though he was past age-and Sarah herself was barren-was enabled to become a father because he considered him faithful who had made the promise. ¹²And so from this one man, and he as good as dead, came descendants as numerous as the stars in the sky and as countless as the sand on the seashore.

11:7 I wonder what Mrs. Noah thought when Mr. Noah took over the front yard to build an ark—and it took him 100 years to finish? Remember that Noah had never seen rain, so he had to walk in total faith and obedience to what he thought God was saying to him.

Can you imagine the ridicule he encountered from those around him, perhaps even from his family, as he proceeded to build according to God's plans and instructions? You may want to review his story found in Genesis 6-9.

11:8-10 God doesn't owe you a full explanation of what's ahead or where you are going when He directs you to do something. If He did owe you that, He would have to apologize to Abraham, whom He ordered to leave his family and set out on a journey to an unknown place. If you had a full explanation, you wouldn't need faith and without faith, it is impossible to please God. Therefore, God only gives as much information as you need today and expects you to trust Him for tomorrow's information.

Faith makes for an amazing study. That is why I wrote what I call *The Faith Files*, a three-volume devotional study of every verse about faith in the New Testament. These books are available to order online in paper or electronic versions.

Think of Abraham's faith. He had to leave the land God had given him by faith on two occasions due to drought. He had to purchase a piece of "his land" in order to bury his wife. Any time he was discouraged, God would have him look at the stars and promise that his descendants would be more numerous than those very stars—all this while he was old and childless. Yes, faith is a fascinating study, but it must be more than a study. Faith is not a study or an event—it is a way of life. It never takes any less faith to grow and move on in God—it always requires more.

As for verse 10, let's look at what Adam Clarke had to say in his commentary:

> [**For he looked for a city which hath foundations**] He knew that earth could afford no

permanent residence for an immortal mind, and he looked for that heavenly building of which God is the architect and owner; in a word, he lost sight of earth, that he might keep heaven in view. And all who are partakers of his faith possess the same spirit, walk by the same rule, and mind the same thing.

[Whose builder and maker is God.] The word *technitees* (**NT:5079**) signifies an architect, one who plans, calculates, and constructs a building. The word *deemiourgos* (**NT:1217**) signifies the governor of a people; one who forms them by institutions and laws; the framer of a political constitution. God is here represented the Maker or Father of all the heavenly inhabitants, and the planner of their citizenship in that heavenly country. (from Adam Clarke's Commentary, Electronic Database. Copyright (c) 1996 by Biblesoft)

Are you a pilgrim, aware that you are looking for another city beyond the one in which you now reside? Have you lost sight of earth because heaven's light is so bright? May the faith of Abraham reside in your heart and may you act in obedience according to that faith. Amen.

11:11-12

Sarah and Abraham weren't just facing old age; Sarah had also been unable to conceive, even in her younger years. They had two strikes against them, but they had God's promise with them and God's promises can overcome any human deficiency or weakness on their way to fulfillment. **What is your focus? Your problem or your promise?** If it's your problem or lack, then you need to shift your focus. Consider what Paul wrote about Abraham:

Therefore, the promise comes by faith, so that it

may be by grace and may be guaranteed to all Abraham's offspring-not only to those who are of the law but also to those who are of the faith of Abraham. He is the father of us all. As it is written: "I have made you a father of many nations."

He is our father in the sight of God, in whom he believed-the God who gives life to the dead and calls things that are not as though they were. Against all hope, Abraham in hope believed and so became the father of many nations, just as it had been said to him, "So shall your offspring be." Without weakening in his faith, he faced the fact that his body was as good as dead-since he was about a hundred years old-and that Sarah's womb was also dead. Yet he did not waver through unbelief regarding the promise of God, but was strengthened in his faith and gave glory to God, being fully persuaded that God had power to do what he had promised.

This is why "it was credited to him as righteousness." The words "it was credited to him" were written not for him alone, but also for us, to whom God will credit righteousness-for us who believe in him who raised Jesus our Lord from the dead. He was delivered over to death for our sins and was raised to life for our justification (Romans 4:16-25).

How can you apply this passage to your life today? What faith lessons can you learn and apply from Abraham? Where are you weakening in faith because you are focusing on the wrong perspective?

¹³All these people were still living by faith

> when they died. They did not receive the things promised; they only saw them and welcomed them from a distance. And they admitted that they were aliens and strangers on earth. ¹⁴People who say such things show that they are looking for a country of their own. ¹⁵If they had been thinking of the country they had left, they would have had opportunity to return. ¹⁶Instead, they were longing for a better country—a heavenly one. Therefore God is not ashamed to be called their God, for he has prepared a city for them.

11:13 This verse tells us it is possible to die in faith, not receiving the things for which we were believing. I decided years ago that I would rather die in faith than live in un-faith or presumption. I figure that, after I die, there is another age when God can "settle all faith accounts." I am making every effort to keep my trust in God, since trust and faith are choices, not dependent on how I feel or what I see around me.

11:14-16 We are citizens of a heavenly Kingdom, looking for something "better" than this earthly life can provide:

> For he has rescued us from the dominion of darkness and brought us into the kingdom of the Son he loves, in whom we have redemption, the forgiveness of sins (Colossians 1:12-14).

When we walk in faith, the ground rules for our lives are different than the rules of un-faith. And we always have a choice to change allegiance. We can return at any time to our lives of un-faith as a citizen of the kingdom of darkness and still go to church and sing hymns. God is not ashamed to be called the God of those who endure the mocking and misunderstanding that a life of faith brings. God has prepared a place to live for those who have put their trust in Him.

I have seen many people get tired of having faith and look to return to a less stressful, more predictable lifestyle. Their salvation isn't in question, but their lifestyle is. **Are you a bit weary right now, tired of not knowing where you are going or your source of provision?** Dear reader, the answer is not less faith, but more. Put your faith in God today and every day. Wait for Him and His provision. He has never failed anyone and He will not ruin His perfect record on you. Keep looking for a better city and resist the temptation to return to the city from whence you came.

> [17] By faith Abraham, when God tested him, offered Isaac as a sacrifice. He who had received the promises was about to sacrifice his one and only son, [18] even though God had said to him, "It is through Isaac that your offspring will be reckoned." [19] Abraham reasoned that God could raise the dead, and figuratively speaking, he did receive Isaac back from death.

11:17-18 You may want to start by reading Genesis 22, the account of Abraham's sacrifice of Isaac. I was in Israel years ago and saw a sculptor's rendition of this sacrifice that changed my way of viewing this story. I had always pictured Isaac bound and laying flat on an altar or rock with Abraham poised above him, ready to plunge a knife into Isaac's chest. This sculptor depicted Abraham standing behind Isaac, who was sitting up and ready to slit his throat. That made sense to me, since Old Testament priests cut the throat of the sacrifices to drain the blood from their bodies before being burned or consumed.

Can you imagine being ready to cut your only son's throat at God's command? I certainly cannot, but that's just what Abraham was ready to do in faith. Having received Isaac in faith, Abraham could not see the promises of God concerning Isaac be fulfilled in any way except ongoing faith. He could not protect his faith child in his own strength. He had to continue to put his trust in God, even if that meant giving back to God what God had given him. You can see why Abraham is the father of anyone who has faith. He was not a perfect man, but he certainly was a man of faith.

God will test your faith. The word "test" here is not the word we use for a school exam. The word *test* here is used in the context of testing metal to prove its purity. God tested Abraham by proving the reality and strength of his faith in God for all generations to see. When God tests you, it isn't to make you stumble. It is rather to show the reality of what He has done in your life.

Think of a recent test you went through; then think of how you would have responded ten years ago. The fact that you kept your trust in God proves the validity of what God has done in your life. The test only proved God's faithfulness. You have no need to fear any test, for it is God revealing even to principalities and powers (and to you and others) what He has put into you by His grace and your consent. Praise God!

11:19 You cannot give something to God in order to preserve it. You cannot think, "I will give this to God and that will preserve it for me because He would *never* allow this to happen." Abraham did not know whether he would ever see Isaac again; Abraham simply put his trust in God. When you give something back to God, He may take and keep it. He then will reward your faithfulness, however, perhaps in ways you cannot imagine. Recently I surrendered my reputation to God and He took it! What's more, it has been tarnished in the taking. I have put my trust in the One who is just and He is free to do with it whatever He wishes. I have chosen to trust Him. **Will you join me in that decision for your own life?**

> [20]By faith Isaac blessed Jacob and Esau in regard to their future. [21]By faith Jacob, when he was dying, blessed each of Joseph's sons, and worshiped as he leaned on the top of his staff. [22]By faith Joseph, when his end was near, spoke about the exodus of the Israelites from Egypt and gave instructions about his bones.

11:20 The story in Genesis 27 is a fascinating one, outlining the intrigue and conniving that surrounded the blessing Isaac gave Jacob when Isaac thought he was giving it to Esau. The writer here attributed the blessing to faith, although it was mixed with human contrivance. Faith never exists in a perfect environment. We humans are all too frail and sinful for that. Yet our human imperfection doesn't prevent us from operating in faith, nor does it prevent God from using us for His faith purposes.

Too often I have been guilty of expecting perfection from others and myself. I have adjusted my expectations as I have gotten older. I won't see perfection this side of the Lord's return, and I have had to get accustomed to the fact that God will use people with less than perfect motives and character.

11:21 For some reason, the Holy Spirit chronicled Jacob's entire life for us to study and from which to learn. In Genesis, we follow his exploits, failures, and development from birth to death. On his deathbed, he blessed his grandsons in faith (see Genesis 47 and 48). Prior to that, he connived and plotted his way to wealth and family problems. In spite of all his weaknesses, God identifies Himself as the "God of Abraham, Isaac, and Jacob." That should give us all hope—hope that God can reach, use, and change anyone. What's more, God doesn't "distance" Himself from less-than-perfect people. **If God doesn't do that, why do we? Can the Church be more "particular" than God Himself when it comes to fellowship? Are you guilty of picking and choosing with whom you will bestow the favor of your presence based on how faithful you perceive people to be?**

11:22 Here we see Joseph, Abraham's great grandson, operating in faith. This is the fourth generation including Abraham that was speaking in faith. That's quite an impressive chain of faith. Someone once said that we are only successful when we have built something in and for God that lasts beyond our own lifetime. If that is true, then Abraham, Isaac, and Jacob did something right, for they were part of a multi-generational faith movement. I hope my family will bless God to the fourth generation. **What steps are you taking to ensure that your faith walk will continue to the next generation? What more can you do?**

> ²³By faith Moses' parents hid him for three months after he was born, because they saw he was no ordinary child, and they were not afraid of the king's edict. ²⁴By faith Moses, when he had grown up,

> refused to be known as the son of Pharaoh's daughter. ²⁵He chose to be mistreated along with the people of God rather than to enjoy the pleasures of sin for a short time. ²⁶He regarded disgrace for the sake of Christ as of greater value than the treasures of Egypt, because he was looking ahead to his reward. ²⁷By faith he left Egypt, not fearing the king's anger; he persevered because he saw him who is invisible. ²⁸By faith he kept the Passover and the sprinkling of blood, so that the destroyer of the firstborn would not touch the firstborn of Israel.

11:23 **What did Moses' parents see?** No newborn is that good looking, even though the parents think he or she is. As stated previously, I believe they saw the purpose of God on their son. Even though the law of the land was that all male babies were to be thrown into the Nile (see Exodus 2), they resisted this immoral edict and preserved the eventual savior of their people. What faith! They lived under tremendous pressure, probably even from other parents who had complied and drowned their sons. Yet they had faith where their son was concerned and God used their faith to preserve His chosen leader. Moses' parents were more afraid of God than Pharaoh; they had their priorities in order. **Do you? Is obedience and pleasing God your top priority, or are there other relationships that have the highest place?**

11:24 **Did you notice that everyone in this Hebrews 11 faith list did something with their faith?** Go back and see what they did. Abraham offered, Isaac blessed, Jacob blessed and worshiped, Moses' parents hid, and Moses refused. This reminds me of what

James wrote: "In the same way, faith by itself, if it is not accompanied by action, is dead" (James 2:16-17). Faith without action is absolutely, positively worthless. Faith isn't right doctrine; it is obedient action that springs from right doctrine. **Are you prone to see faith as active or passive, what you believe or what you do?**

In this verse, faith required that Moses deny all the comforts and connections of being the adopted son of Pharaoh's daughter to identify with the lowly estate of his people's slavery in Egypt. **What faith steps can you take today to walk out what you believe?**

11:25 I have a friend who has a ministry to young people through which he talks about drug abuse. He can do this because he abused drugs and that abuse contributed to him taking the life of another person. In his presentation, he says that drugs do give something, but what they take is not worth what they give. There is wisdom in this perspective. Too often the Church has acted like sin is without pleasure and must be avoided. The problem is that there is pleasure in sin and to deny or ignore that is to lose a chance to identify with the audience to whom we are preaching. This verse says there *is* pleasure in sin, but it is passing or fleeting.

Moses chose to endure mistreatment instead of the passing pleasure. That is often the price of leadership for anyone and it certainly was for Moses. He made the right choice, however, and that choice helped shape him into one of the world's most famous leaders. **What price are you paying for leadership? What choices are you making today that will make you a better leader tomorrow?**

Every morning, I begin my day by writing this Bible study or my daily online devotional. I choose not to do something else during that time so I can write, and any leadership is made up of a series of similar decisions. You must decide what price you are willing to pay to be an effective leader. I urge you today to make good choices and deny some gratification that will lead to greater effectiveness tomorrow.

11:26 It is of note that the writer equated Moses' decision not to be known as Pharaoh's nephew as enduring disgrace for the sake of Christ, and that happened about 1,700 years prior to Christ's birth. Somehow God had made known to Moses His plan to send a Messiah from among Moses' people. This revelation was so clear that Moses focused his whole life and decisions on the truth of what God had shown him.

If Moses could focus his entire life and "career" on the reality of Christ, how much more should we do the same? When you think of it, Moses did choose his "career" based on the reality of Christ. **Are you doing the same? Have you made decisions about your future that were based on what was best for you, or have you made those decisions based on what Jesus would have you do?** Moses was looking ahead to his reward. **Are you making decisions on what is best for you now or what is best for you in the long run?** While God is not opposed to politics, He is opposed to politics that causes anyone to take moral shortcuts for the expediency of a promotion, a raise, or related benefits. **Moses "put it all on the line" for Jesus; can you do any less?**

11:27 Faith always affects what you see. Moses looked through the anger and threats of the king he could see, because he saw the reality of the King whom he could not see. Moses based his decisions not on the shifting sands of the seen, but on the solid rock of faith, the unseen. **What are you looking at today? Are you**

looking at what anyone can see or what only a few can see through the eyes of faith?

I implore you to join with Moses and make your decisions today and every day based on your unwavering focus on Jesus. Don't be swayed by what others say they see; walk in the reality of what God is showing you. Don't be afraid of news reports, family pressures, or cultural wisdom concerning your job, ministry, or professional development.

11:28 The first Passover is described in Exodus 12. At that time, most families put their trust in the continuation of their family line and name in the oldest son, who represented the future. The Egyptians worshiped this firstborn (especially the firstborn of Pharaoh who was considered a god) as they did most of creation (the plagues came to destroy the Egyptian confidence in all their so-called gods). Moses and the Jews did not put their trust in this family custom of the firstborn, but rather they put their trust in God. The judgment of God came against all those in Egypt who put their trust in anything or anyone but Him.

I am glad I have applied the blood of the Lamb to the doorpost of my home where we have lived within the safety and protection of that blood. I have not put my faith in a doctrine, denomination, or my own credentials or education. I have put my faith in God just like Moses did, and He is faithful. **Is that your testimony as well?**

> [29] By faith the people passed through the Red Sea as on dry land; but when the Egyptians tried to do so, they were drowned. [30] By faith the walls of Jericho fell, after the people had marched around them for seven days. [31] By faith the prostitute Rahab, because she welcomed the spies,

was not killed with those who were disobedient.

11:29 No one can imitate someone else's faith. The Egyptians did not know God and tried to imitate the faith of the Jews. They drowned in their own presumption trying to cross the Red Sea. It is one thing to be optimistic and confident, but if your confidence isn't in God, then it is just an exercise in futility. When you are walking through dangerous territory, you had better base your confidence not on the words of your government, your church, or your family. You had better base your confidence on God's word.

When I was in Afghanistan years ago, I experienced more pressure and spiritual warfare than usual, as would be expected. I had to know every day that I was hearing from God and putting my faith in what I thought He was saying to me. My ability to do so saved my life; it wasn't just a matter of convenience. We found out there was a conspiracy to commit violent acts against us the entire time we were there.

11:30 How many times did Joshua and Israel walk around Jericho? If you said seven times, you are incorrect (see Joshua 6). They walked around once a day for six days, then they walked around the city seven times on the seventh day. That makes 13 times. What a "silly" strategy, carried out while they were not permitted to talk to one another as they walked. Maybe that was so they would not discuss the foolishness of what they were doing and undermine one another's faith.

God can show you strategies of how your business can prosper, ministry can expand, or opposition be defeated. First, however, you must have faith that He can and will do what He has promised. Then you must have faith to carry out those strategies out, even when they seem unusual to you and to others.

When I was a counselor, whenever I would meet with someone in my church, I would usually ask, "What is the Lord saying?" I wanted to know what they thought they were sensing and hearing; then I based my counsel on their response. God is a great communicator. He knows every language, can speak through circumstances, His word, other believers, non-believers, and even a donkey. **What is God saying to you today? Are you being faithful to what you think it is?** May the walls of your Jericho come down as you carry out in faith the plans God has laid before you.

11:31 How did Rahab know who the spies were? (See Joshua 2 and 6). There was only one way—God "told" or revealed them to her. There are some who don't think Rahab was a harlot, but rather an innkeeper. Whatever her occupation, God revealed His plan to her *before* she had a change of lifestyle or was part of the covenant community. She put her trust in God and she and her whole family were saved. What's more, Rahab became a part of Jesus' family tree (see Matthew 1:5). Thus, she was a precursor of the faith made available to the Gentiles in Christ.

God delights in revealing Himself to people who don't appear to be likely candidates for such a revelation. The Church has not always delighted, however, in this aspect of God's character of mercy and grace. **How do you feel when someone you don't think is worthy of God finds God?** When I was regularly speaking in prisons, I found myself ministering to a new convert who was in prison for murdering his parents in a drug-crazed frenzy. There he was, sitting at my feet, "clothed and in his right mind." I was angry that this man had found Jesus and I struggled ministering to him. Then I thought, "If Jesus doesn't have a problem with this man, then I shouldn't either."

The Church sometimes gets angry when homosexuals, child abusers, prostitutes, persecutors, and drug dealers find Jesus. The message of Rahab, however, is that God reveals Himself to whomever He chooses and doesn't ask anyone's permission to do so.

Is there some unlikely candidate to whom God wants to reveal Himself today, using you in the process? If so, will you cooperate or have a bad attitude? I hope you will cooperate and spread the good news of Jesus to any and all. Remember, Jesus didn't come for the well but for the sick and wants to make us outreach doctors in His image. I hope we will be up to the task.

> [32] And what more shall I say? I do not have time to tell about Gideon, Barak, Samson, Jephthah, David, Samuel and the prophets, [33] who through faith conquered kingdoms, administered justice, and gained what was promised; who shut the mouths of lions, [34] quenched the fury of the flames, and escaped the edge of the sword; whose weakness was turned to strength; and who became powerful in battle and routed foreign armies. [35] Women received back their dead, raised to life again. Others were tortured and refused to be released, so that they might gain a better resurrection. [36] Some faced jeers and flogging, while still others were chained and put in prison. [37] They were stoned; they were sawed in two; they were put

> to death by the sword. They went about in sheepskins and goatskins, destitute, persecuted and mistreated—³⁸the world was not worthy of them. They wandered in deserts and mountains, and in caves and holes in the ground. ³⁹These were all commended for their faith, yet none of them received what had been promised. ⁴⁰God had planned something better for us so that only together with us would they be made perfect.

11:32 When the author started to write about faith, he simply had too much material, so he had to bring this portion of the letter to a close. The Bible is full of stories of men and women who put their faith in God and saw results worthy of being recorded for future generations. It is only what we do in faith that is worthy of such a legacy. When the writer wrote "what more shall I say?', it has led some to believe that this letter to the Hebrews was originally a sermon transcribed into written form.

Three names strike me as odd on the list in this verse: Barak, Samson, and Jephthah. Barak was conscripted into the deliverance of Israel by the prophetess Deborah. I refer to him as the reluctant warrior (see Judges 4). Jephthah was another warrior, but he endured much scorn because he was the son of a prostitute (see Judges 11-12), yet God used him to deliver Israel. Samson had a major character flaw in his relationships with women, but God used him nonetheless to bring down the Philistines (see Judges 13-16). The stories of these three men should encourage you that if God can use them in His work, then God can also use *you* to do His work and will, regardless of your flaws and failures.

11:33-34 These great faith heroes did mighty exploits. It seems that one phrase in particular, however, is worthy of special attention. It says they *became* powerful in battle. Most of us want to be powerful and then enter into battle. These heroes, however, didn't find their power *until* they entered battle. That is real faith—to not "feel" anything special, but still move at the direction of God's word. When you move in that kind of obedient faith, *then* and *only then* does God gives you the strength you need. It proves once again that faith without some kind of action is useless, for your strength is not activated by your faith, but by acting on your faith.

It also says that their "weakness was turned to strength." Don't wait until you have the strength you think you will need. Act and trust that God will give you the strength when you need it. As usual, I must ask you: **How can you apply this truth to your life today? Not next week, or next month, but *today*? Where have you been waiting for some supernatural boost but now realize it is your actions that will activate and provide this boost?**

11:35-36 Apart from the two sons that Elijah and Elisha brought back to life, I am not sure what the writer was referring to in this verse. The point is, however, that faith doesn't guarantee an outcome everyone would consider as acceptable. Here we read that some were walking in faith and because of faith were tortured, flogged, jeered, and imprisoned.

It is difficult to hold on to faith in the midst of unpleasant or difficult circumstances. As stated earlier, study, however, it seems preferable and more noble to die in faith than to live in un-faith or presumption. There are some who have tried to use faith as a means to control the circumstances in their lives so they can avoid pain, suffering, or confusion. Faith isn't something you use to that end. Faith is a way of life that ultimately says, "Lord, I trust You, no matter what happens. I know what I see is a limited perspective, so I am putting my trust in what You see and allow to happen. I trust You know what You are doing."

Church tradition tells us that almost all the original apostles died a martyr's death. **Did they lack faith?** Some may say they did. I would prefer to conclude their faith allowed them to fulfill the truth found in Revelation:

> "They overcame him by the blood of the Lamb and by the word of their testimony; they did not love their lives so much as to shrink from death" (Revelation 12:11).

Their deaths, and the deaths of so many martyrs, did not represent unbelief, but the ultimate expression of faith and confidence. It seems that miracles often happen not for those who have faith, but for those who do not. You see, if someone has faith, they don't need the miracles to stand firm. They already have a conviction of what cannot be seen—they have the reward for their faith.

It is those who are weak in faith who need the miracles or confirmations. **Isn't that how Jesus used miracles? Was it not to strengthen or establish faith in those with whom He was working? And then once they had faith, did they not go and perform their own miracles for the benefit of other unbelievers?**

11:37 This list is not exactly an advertisement for the life of faith. We cannot be sure of the stories the writer was thinking about when he composed this list of trials, but it goes back to what we discussed in the previous verses: Faith does not guarantee an easy life or a happy outcome. **You may be inspired by the price others have paid to walk out their faith, but are you willing to pay**

that price yourself? The way to please God is not through someone else's faith, however, but through our own. **Are there stories and lives that inspire you to faith? What are they? Is it time to review them? Is it time to write your own faith story that will inspire others?**

11:38 The world sees the people described in this passage as misfits and failures. It is ironic that these are the very people whom God honors because their rejection by the world was based on their faith in God. Faith may not earn you a parade in this life, but the Bible promises an awards ceremony in the next life that will bestow honors on everyone who put their trust in God. **When do you want your parade: now or later?** The answer to that question will determine how you invest your life now. Jesus talked about this principle when He said,

> "Do not store up for yourselves treasures on earth, where moths and vermin destroy, and where thieves break in and steal. But store up for yourselves treasures in heaven, where moths and vermin do not destroy, and where thieves do not break in and steal" (Matthew 6:19-20).

Where are you storing up treasures—in the now or in the hereafter?

11:39 Each person mentioned in the preceding verses was commended. **Who commended them?** It had to be God. **And how did He commend them?** We really don't know, except that some of their stories are included in His inspired Word. Others received praise they knew was from God but perhaps no one else did. Consider what was written in John's gospel:

> "I do not accept praise from men, but I know you. I know that you do not have the love of

God in your hearts. I have come in my Father's name, and you do not accept me; but if someone else comes in his own name, you will accept him. How can you believe if you accept praise from one another, yet make no effort to obtain the praise that comes from the only God?" (John 5:41-44).

God knows how to encourage and reward His servants in ways special to them alone. **What are you willing to do to be commended by God? How will you feel if your commendation is not seen or recognized by other people, even those who are closest to you?**

11:40 While each person commended in Hebrews 11 had faith in God, they did not receive what was promised, because Jesus was the ultimate promise. My ultimate faith reward is to know Jesus and to be like Him. The object of my faith cannot be houses, cars, ministries, or spiritual gifts. While all those things may come, the ultimate reward was and is to know and be known by Jesus. **Is that your ultimate goal as well?**

The Catholic Church refers to as the "communion of the saints." This communion is realized as each one of us takes our place next to those who have gone before us as we put our faith in God through Christ. Faith is the common denominator defining our communion with those of the past, present, and future. It is not about what individual church we belong to; it is the fact that we are part of *the* Church by faith.

12

> Therefore, since we are surrounded by such a great cloud of witnesses, let us throw off everything that hinders and the sin that so easily entangles, and let us run with perseverance the race marked out for us. ²Let us fix our eyes on Jesus, the author and perfecter of our faith, who for the joy set before him endured the cross, scorning its shame, and sat down at the right hand of the throne of God. ³Consider him who endured such opposition from sinful men, so that you will not grow weary and lose heart.

12:1 The image used by the writer here is one of an Olympic race where many bystanders are watching the runner exert himself to win. The "therefore" in this verse obviously ties it back to the stories just written in the preceding chapter. I am not sure we have a literal audience in heaven of the great faith heroes of the past, but we are continuing their faith work in our generation. Against that backdrop, the writer urged us to run the faith race marked out for us.

The faith race is not a sprint, but a marathon requiring patience and perseverance. It is not who starts quickly, nor the one who has a lead at the halfway point who wins the race. And our main enemy in the race is sin, which so conveniently wraps itself around us to slow us down or knock us out of the race. **How are you doing in the race set before you? Are you running to win or is sin weighing you down, hindering your ability to compete?**

12:2 **What can we do to help us win the race?** As much as the heroes of Hebrews 11 can encourage and help, there is only one source of strength and motivation for the faith race, and that help is Jesus. Abraham, Moses, and the others can provide us encouragement as we read about their lives, but Jesus helps us not only through the story of His life, but also through the power of the Holy Spirit. We are commanded to "fix our eyes" on Jesus. **How can we see someone who cannot be seen?** Only through faith eyes. Remember what we learned from Hebrews 11—that faith *always* leads to vision.

What do you see? What is your vision for your life and those around you? What are you building and growing for God in the way of ministry or fruit? What you see is what you get when it comes to faith. When you think of it, the ultimate faith expression was Jesus' life, as expressed by His death, burial, and resurrection. Jesus isn't asking you to do anything He hasn't already done, which is go put your complete and total trust in God. That is why you can and should study the lives of the faith heroes, but you must fix your faith eyes on Jesus, the faith champion.

12:3 The original readers of Hebrews must have encountered tremendous and unrelenting opposition from their fellow Jews who were unbelievers. The writer reminded them their opposition was similar to what

Jesus experienced. Jesus endured and accomplished the will of the Father and because He did, we can do it too.

If you see Jesus as some divine superhero, you forfeit His ability to help you in the race you are running. If you see Jesus as a human being like you (except without sin), then you can call on Him to help you in times of trouble because He has been where you are. **Are you calling on Jesus for help? Are you drawing all the help you can not only from His example but also from His divine grace He gives freely? Where can you rely more fully and completely on Jesus?**

> ⁴In your struggle against sin, you have not yet resisted to the point of shedding your blood. ⁵And you have forgotten that word of encouragement that addresses you as sons: "My son, do not make light of the Lord's discipline, and do not lose heart when he rebukes you, ⁶because the Lord disciplines those he loves, and he punishes everyone he accepts as a son."

12:4

There is one word in this verse that catches my attention, and that is the word *yet*. I wish I could ask the writer, "What do you mean I haven't *yet* resisted to the point of shedding blood?" Of course, I am having a little fun here, for I know the main point of the verse is to highlight the fact that Jesus shed His blood in the battle against sin. No matter how badly I may have it in this life, I cannot even begin to approach what Jesus did until I give my life; and even then, my sacrifice cannot be compared to His.

The writer shifted the attention to Jesus as he concluded his discussion of faith. If you are encountering opposition from sinful people or struggling with sin in your own life, do not give in to discouragement or self-pity. What's more, you cannot compare what you are going through to anyone else's situation. You must compare what you are going through to what Jesus went through. That is the only standard you are permitted to have. When you compare, you will see that there is no comparison.

12:5-6 Some of the struggles you are going through may be forms of God's discipline. It is a sign of God's love and not His anger or displeasure when you encounter this kind of discipline. The writer quoted Proverbs 3:11-12 in this verse, which appeared to be an admonition from David or Solomon to one of their sons. While they were writing to their own sons, they were really writing a divinely-inspired message from God to His children.

We are God's children and we must never lose sight of that fact. Because we are His children, He must act as our Father and at times chasten, rebuke, or discipline us. This is the only explanation for some of what you are going through right now. The lack of finances, the job that doesn't allow you to utilize all your gifts and talents, the relationship that isn't what you want it to be—all these can be forms of discipline. If you see them as signs of God's love for you, however, it can change how you view and react to them.

Where is God disciplining you right now? Are you joyfully enduring it? Can you thank Him for it?

> [7]Endure hardship as discipline; God is treating you as sons. For what son is not disciplined by his father? [8]If you are not disciplined (and everyone undergoes discipline), then you are illegitimate

children and not true sons. ⁹Moreover, we have all had human fathers who disciplined us and we respected them for it. How much more should we submit to the Father of our spirits and live! ¹⁰Our fathers disciplined us for a little while as they thought best; but God disciplines us for our good, that we may share in his holiness. ¹¹No discipline seems pleasant at the time, but painful. Later on, however, it produces a harvest of righteousness and peace for those who have been trained by it. ¹²Therefore, strengthen your feeble arms and weak knees. ¹³"Make level paths for your feet," so that the lame may not be disabled, but rather healed.

12:7 The command in this verse is for you to endure; the incentive to endure is that what you are going through is not from the devil or your own decisions. What you are going through is from God. The writer drew on an earthly analogy of fathers who discipline their earthly children, something to which many readers can relate.

12:8 God's discipline is a sign of legitimacy. The hardship you are going through is proof of God's love for you, because He is training you in His ways. God loves you enough even to endure your misunderstanding as He disciplines you for your good and to make you more like Him. It also increases your trust and faith in Him as you grow through the trials and discipline to learn obedience and understand new depths of God's grace.

12:9 I have counseled many people who had little discipline from earthly parents and they struggle with rejection. They interpreted the lack of discipline to mean their parents didn't love them and not to mean their parents loved them so much that they couldn't discipline them. **If you are a parent, are you willing to endure the misunderstanding of your children as you discipline them? If you are a child, can you see your parent's discipline as a sign of love and not control or meanness?**

Ultimately, can you as a child of God see your current circumstances as a sign of God's love and not anything else? If you are a child of God, can you see your Father's love and hand in your life right now? Can you trust that you have not done something wrong, but that God is working in and with you to train you for some future good? I hope you can. Submit to your heavenly Father's hand of discipline and read on, for this discipline will not last forever.

12:10 The goal of God's discipline for us is to share in His holiness. God knows what He is doing and disciplines us with perfection, even though at times, it may not seem like there is a reason for what is happening in our lives. That is where faith comes in, for we can be certain that there is—a reason that is based in love and God's perfect justice.

One thing you will never hear God say is "I'm sorry." He never apologizes for what He does or what He puts you through, for His ways are perfect—there is nothing to apologize for. You must be careful not to think or accuse God of being unjust or unloving. If He is, that would make you more righteous than God and that is not a possibility.

If you had a less than pleasant experiences with your earthly father, you must be careful not to project that bad experience onto God and His Fatherhood. Your earthly parents were and are imperfect, some painfully so, but you must now learn to trust your heavenly Father and His discipline in your life. **Are you struggling with trusting God in the midst of your current struggles?** Then tell Him and ask Him for grace, not to understand, but to release your perspective to Him so you can trust.

12:11 Discipline is seldom enjoyable. You don't have to enjoy the season of discipline you may be in. Accept it in faith, confess that the destination is worth the price you are paying, and ask God's grace to endure the season you are in. I am thinking of some verses in Thessalonians, which state, "Be joyful always; pray continually; give thanks in all circumstances, for this is God's will for you in Christ Jesus" (1 Thessalonians 5:16-18).

Paul did not say to give thanks *for* all things, but *in* all things. Seasons of discipline are certainly times *in* which we give thanks, but not necessarily *for* which we give thanks. **Can you thank God now in the midst of what you are going through? Can you find other blessings on which to focus while certain other parts of your life seem to be spinning out of control or playing out in ways not to your liking?**

By the way, the word *trained* in this verse is the Greek word from which we get our word *gymnasium*. All this talk of discipline reminds me of athletic training. The athlete endures many hours of rigorous training for an athletic performance. It is the same for the believer who must also endure much training to be mature enough for God to use him or her.

12:12-13 There is no room for self-pity in this spiritual "athletic" preparation. You cannot allow yourself the luxury of feeling sorry for yourself in what you are going through. The writer, who was addressing believing Jews who were undoubtedly enduring hardship for their faith, was telling these believers to strengthen themselves, to "get on with their lives," so to speak. **Are you wallowing in self-pity right now? Do you think you have earned the right to do so?** Paul warned us that there are many hardships the Christian must endure:

> They preached the good news in that city and won a large number of disciples. Then they returned to Lystra, Iconium and Antioch, strengthening the disciples and encouraging them to remain true to the faith. "We must go through many hardships to enter the kingdom of God," they said (Acts 14:21-22).

The news that there are many hardships may not encourage some people. You may encounter things in your walk with the Lord that cause you to stumble. Even those who walked with Jesus heard Him say things that caused those people to withdraw (see John 6). It is possible for your limbs to be out of joint, so to speak, as you walk out your faith.

If you are discouraged or perhaps a bit disillusioned at this point in your walk with God, then these verses in chapter 12 are for you. You need to strengthen yourself and move on. If you are limping, then get those joints back in place. I know this may be easier said than done, and I certainly don't know what you have been through. God knows, however, and He will help you. You must do your part, which is to choose to move on and get through this season of training and discipline.

You may not know where all this is leading to, but you can take solace in the fact that if you endure, you will share in God's holiness when all is said and done. May God strengthen you today and may you walk on with grace and peace.

¹⁴Make every effort to live in peace with

all men and to be holy; without holiness no one will see the Lord. ¹⁵See to it that no one misses the grace of God and that no bitter root grows up to cause trouble and defile many. ¹⁶See that no one is sexually immoral, or is godless like Esau, who for a single meal sold his inheritance rights as the oldest son. ¹⁷Afterward, as you know, when he wanted to inherit this blessing, he was rejected. He could bring about no change of mind, though he sought the blessing with tears.

12:14 It can be difficult to be at peace with others due to our fallen nature; it takes effort. We have to do very little for war to break out between friends while working hard to maintain peace with other people, even those closest to us. Paul wrote, "If it is possible, as far as it depends on you, live at peace with everyone" (Romans 12:18). In regards to peace with others, Jesus said,

> "Therefore, if you are offering your gift at the altar and there remember that your brother has something against you, leave your gift there in front of the altar. First go and be reconciled to your brother; then come and offer your gift" (Matthew 5:23-24).

You must also work at being holy in your relationships if you want to see the Lord. Remember what Jesus said. "Blessed are the pure in heart, for they will see God" (Matthew 5:8). **Is there anyone with whom you need to be diligent to maintain peace between the two of you? Is there anyone with whom you need to make peace and start over, so to speak, to keep a peaceful relationship?**

12:15 Bitterness is poison, pure and simple. Bitterness affects not only the one who is bitter, but also many others related to the people close to you. **Are you bitter? Are you around anyone who is? What affect is this having on you right now? Is there anything you can do to remove or lessen the bitterness?**

12:16-17 You must not interpret these verses to mean that Esau was sexually immoral. Rather he sold his birthright for what was next to nothing: a pot of stew (see Genesis 25:29). When he realized what he had done, he didn't really repent of his ways; he simply wept over the consequences of what he had done. There is a difference between being sorry and repentance. **What is that difference? Can someone cry over what they have done and not repent?**

The lesson here is that you should not sell or forfeit your spiritual heritage and privileges for something that is here today and gone tomorrow. You must learn to sacrifice temporary pleasure for what provides an eternal reward.

> [18] You have not come to a mountain that can be touched and that is burning with fire; to darkness, gloom and storm; [19] to a trumpet blast or to such a voice speaking words that those who heard it begged that no further word be spoken to them, [20] because they could not bear what was commanded: "If even an animal touches the mountain, it must be stoned." [21] The sight was so terrifying that Moses said, "I am trembling with fear."

12:18-21 The Law was an awe-inspiring and often terrifying thing. Of course, this reference is found in Exodus 19:12-13 and refers to the mountain where Moses received the Law. Even Moses, who was intimate with God, was fearful when he faced the scenario of receiving the Law from the hand and mouth of God. The writer has returned in these verses to the theme of comparing the Law with the dispensation of grace produced by Jesus' life and ministry. Remember that some reading this letter were believing Jews who were considering a return to Judaism. The writer was simply telling them that the Law was a serious and fearful entity, but the new Law of the New Testament is more awesome still— and worthy of their devotion and focus.

Have you known people who are tired of the unpredictability of faith and long for the more predictable ways of a previous religious experience or system? Are you tired of faith? Don't romanticize the past; the good old days were never that good. Compared to the difficulty you are in now, however, those past days may seem to have provided a better, more stable way of life. You need to move on, not move back. **Is there any area of your life where you are yearning for those good old days, thus robbing you of the treasures to be found in this new day?**

There are some who think, "If only God would speak to me, then I would know or move or do." Yet when God spoke to those in Exodus 19, they changed their minds and said, "Let Him talk to Moses and we will listen to him, our leader." The voice of God was a terrifying thing for those who heard it.

What's more, it is an easy thing to look past what God may be saying to other voices out of ignorance, wrong thinking, or hard-heartedness. That is why the Word is important. You need to study and listen to its warnings, lessons, and admonitions. The inner voice you hear can sound much like your own and thus subject you to your own limitations as you try to comprehend and process what you hear.

Peter and a few apostles heard the voice of God on the Mount of Transfiguration, yet this was Peter's conclusion about that episode as he wrote in his second epistle:

> He received honor and glory from God the Father when the voice came to him from the Majestic Glory, saying, "This is my Son, whom I love; with him I am well pleased." We ourselves heard this voice that came from heaven when we were with him on the sacred mountain. We also have the prophetic message as something completely reliable, and you will do well to pay attention to it, as to a light shining in a dark place, until the day dawns and the morning star rises in your hearts (2 Peter 1:17-19).

Peter was saying that he heard the voice but came to realize the prophetic message contained in God's word is completely reliable and capable of speaking to us about our daily situations.

> [22]But you have come to Mount Zion, to the heavenly Jerusalem, the city of the living God. You have come to thousands upon thousands of angels in joyful assembly, [23]to the church of the firstborn, whose names are written in heaven. You have come to God, the judge of all men, to the spirits of righteous men made perfect, [24]to Jesus the mediator of a new covenant, and to the sprinkled blood that speaks a better word than the blood of Abel.

12:22 The Law is compared to the new Law under Jesus. The Law was presented to a group of people near a mountain; the Gospel created a new city inhabited by people of faith. **I would rather live in a city than at the base of a terrifying mountain, wouldn't you?** There are thousands of angels overseeing the heavenly city as opposed to the few angels who instituted the Law on the mountain (see Galatians 3:19).

12:23 The firstborn members of this gospel city have their names written in heaven. The firstborn of Israel had their names recorded in their family genealogy. I would rather have a good name registered in heaven than one registered on earth. We are heavenly citizens. If someone wants to be more than that, they will have to settle for an earthly religious system that gives honor now as opposed to a heavenly, invisible one that gives honor to its citizens later. **Which one do you want? Do you want your honor now, or are you willing to work to store up treasure in heaven so you can receive your honor later, as Jesus advised you to do?**

> "Do not store up for yourselves treasures on earth, where moths and vermin destroy, and where thieves break in and steal. But store up for yourselves treasures in heaven, where moths and vermin do not destroy, and where thieves do not break in and steal. For where your treasure is, there your heart will be also" (Matthew 6:19-21).

12:24 Jesus' blood is superior to the blood of any Old Testament sacrifice. What's more, Jesus is a superior mediator of the New Covenant, which is also a better covenant than the old. That makes Jesus superior to Moses, whom the Jews revered. **What could there be in any religious system that is superior to Jesus and His**

"**system?**" There is none, yet men and women regularly choose the inferior to Jesus because of the stigma and unpredictability of faith.

> ²⁵See to it that you do not refuse him who speaks. If they did not escape when they refused him who warned them on earth, how much less will we, if we turn away from him who warns us from heaven? ²⁶At that time his voice shook the earth, but now he has promised, "Once more I will shake not only the earth but also the heavens." ²⁷The words "once more" indicate the removing of what can be shaken-that is, created things-so that what cannot be shaken may remain. ²⁸Therefore, since we are receiving a kingdom that cannot be shaken, let us be thankful, and so worship God acceptably with reverence and awe, ²⁹for our "God is a consuming fire."

12:25 Notice the present tense used in the words *who speaks*. Jesus is always speaking because He is a great communicator. He speaks every language; can talk through circumstances or His Word; can use a believer or non-believer to communicate; and can even speak through a donkey if need be. God is speaking to you right now. It is always important that you focus on what He is saying or else you will look for some old religious experience or system to lead and guide you.

Can you summarize what you think God is "saying" to you at the present time? What is He emphasizing or teaching you? Patience? Generosity? Having you guard your tongue? Be more kind to others? It is important that you pay attention and honor what He is saying. The writer was trying to impress upon the readers that, if the Law had serious penalties for those who refused to listen, there are even more serious ramifications for those who ignore what God is saying now through Jesus.

It is only during the last ten years that I have started to write down what I think God is showing me. In fact, these Bible studies were an attempt to pay closer attention to what I was seeing and learning from God's word. I have never been a good journal-er, but I am trying to improve to pay attention and retain what I hear more effectively. **Is this something you need to do as well? What is stopping you from being more effective at keeping a journal?**

12:26-27 Any man-made system has been, is being, or will be shaken so that the only system that cannot be shaken—the gospel—will remain. **Have you experienced any shaking in your life lately?** If you haven't, you will.

It is easy for us to put our trust in some man-made system, even a system that had its roots in the gospel. In fact, we crave such systems for we want to understand God and how we can make Him work on our behalf, thus trying to control God. God will shake anything in which we put our trust so that we learn to put our trust in ultimate reality and truth, namely Jesus.

I have felt several earth tremors in my travels. That experience was a bit unnerving, but it is much worse to endure the spiritual shaking that can occur when God is proving what is unshakable by shaking everything else. While the shaking isn't always pleasant, it is helpful by allowing us to take refuge in that which will stand forever.

12:28 The implication here is clear: Why would any reader consider living in a kingdom that can be shaken (the Law) when the unshakable kingdom is available (the gospel)? When the shaking comes—and it will come—we need to be thankful that ultimately, we have an unshakable reality in Jesus. **Are you thankful for this fact? Does it lead you to worship Him and give thanks?** If not, it should.

I have found that the shaking can far exceed my expectations, so it is important I am grounded in God and put my trust in Him. If you are going through some shaking, don't be surprised. Run into Jesus, for He is the best refuge available. Don't think you have necessarily done anything wrong, for God may be showing you how firm your grounding is in the shaking. If you need to hold onto something, hold onto Him.

12:29 Without proper protection, those who approach God can be burned up, and that proper protection is holiness. Think of it: Fire has never damaged God's people. They have always come through the fire. It is the unrighteous who cannot stand the fire of God's presence. God is always looking to burn up that which isn't holy or righteous. I wonder if hell isn't some expression of this truth. If we allow God to burn away our impurities now, we have hope. If we wait, then we meet eternal fire that punishes but never purifies. **I would rather the fire that consumes my sin now rather than the one that consumes me later, wouldn't you?**

> But now, this is what the Lord says—he who created you, Jacob, he who formed you, Israel: "Do not fear, for I have redeemed you; I have summoned you by name; you are mine. When you pass through the waters, I will be with you; and when you pass through the rivers, they will not sweep over you. When you walk through the

fire, you will not be burned; the flames will not set you ablaze. For I am the Lord your God, the Holy One of Israel, your Savior" (Isaiah 43:1-3a).

Let's also look at what Peter wrote:

> Praise be to the God and Father of our Lord Jesus Christ! In his great mercy he has given us new birth into a living hope through the resurrection of Jesus Christ from the dead, and into an inheritance that can never perish, spoil or fade-kept in heaven for you, who through faith are shielded by God's power until the coming of the salvation that is ready to be revealed in the last time. In this you greatly rejoice, though now for a little while you may have had to suffer grief in all kinds of trials. These have come so that your faith-of greater worth than gold, which perishes even though refined by fire-may be proved genuine and may result in praise, glory and honor when Jesus Christ is revealed (1 Peter 1:3-8).

The shaking comes to prove the reality and faithfulness of God's unshakable kingdom and presence in your life.

13

Keep on loving each other as brothers. ²Do not forget to entertain strangers, for by so doing some people have entertained angels without knowing it. ³Remember those in prison as if you were their fellow prisoners, and those who are mistreated as if you yourselves were suffering.

13:1 The Bible would not repeatedly tell us to love and forgive one another unless we were often going to need those reminders. Someone once joked that the church would be a great place without people. There may be some truth to that, but the church *is* people, and people can be hard to get along with. Sometimes we don't have to do anything to offend people and others may not even be aware they have offended us. Both Jesus and Paul taught about love and forgiveness. Here are a few of the things they said:

> "Then Peter came to Jesus and asked, 'Lord, how many times shall I forgive my brother when he sins against me? Up to seven times?' Jesus answered, 'I tell you, not seven times, but

seventy-seven times'" (Matthew 18:21-22).

Bear with each other and forgive whatever grievances you may have against one another. Forgive as the Lord forgave you (Colossians 3:12-13).

"So watch yourselves. If your brother or sister sins against you, rebuke them; and if they repent, forgive them" (Luke 17:3).

There have been people who I have found particularly difficult to love. I have had to ask God to help me love them, confessing the reality of my non-love. **Is there anyone who you need supernatural help to love today?**

13:2 This verse addresses the need to be hospitable as a spiritual practice. **How open is your home to others, either for a meal or an overnight stay?** In biblical times, there were few hotels or inns, so traveling saints had to rely on the hospitality of brothers and sisters. Hospitality can be an invasion of your privacy, upsetting your routine and schedule. That may be the very thing that is most valuable about hospitality. It takes you and your family out of the ordinary so you can experience the blessing of giving something intangible to other people—warmth, comfort, and fellowship. Peter also urged the saints in one of his letters to be hospitable: "Offer hospitality to one another without grumbling" (1 Peter 4:9).

Is this what you are doing? How can you show hospitality to someone soon? The two who entertained angels were Abraham and Lot (see Genesis 18:3 and 19:2). They thought the visitors were travelers and instead found themselves entertaining angels. You never know the blessings in store when you open your heart and home to visitors.

13:3 The writer was not referring to prisoners in general, but rather those who were imprisoned for their faith (although there is nothing wrong with applying this to modern prison settings). There was no prison system back then like we are accustomed to today with visitation and other programs. We should extend this principle to visit anyone we may know who is in prison for whatever reason.

I have been in a lot of prisons and the conditions are better than most would expect. The people are lonely and lost and a prison visit is a wonderful place to give something away for which the recipients cannot repay you. Even writing letters to inmates can be an act of mercy to them. And of course, helping the families of those incarcerated is another way to show the love of God to someone who is down and out.

> [4] Marriage should be honored by all, and the marriage bed kept pure, for God will judge the adulterer and all the sexually immoral. [5] Keep your lives free from the love of money and be content with what you have, because God has said, "Never will I leave you; never will I forsake you." [6] So we say with confidence, "The Lord is my helper; I will not be afraid. What can man do to me?" [7] Remember your leaders, who spoke the word of God to you. Consider the outcome of their way of life and imitate their faith. [8] Jesus Christ is the same yesterday and today and forever.

13:4 This seems straightforward, but marriage today is under attack like never before. Same-sex unions, the ease of divorce, the acceptance of cohabitation, Internet pornography, and materialism all work to dishonor and discredit traditional, biblical marriage. The truth is that

God has judged and will judge adulterers and fornicators, but the lax and permissive moral state of modern society makes even that statement of judgment sound harsh.

Yet God's forgiveness extends to the sexually impure, and, in today's culture, it's difficult to find someone who isn't tainted by this plague. The Church needs to maintain a standard of purity, while extending grace and forgiveness to all those who fall short.

13:5 You may be going through rough economic times, just as some of the original readers were. Some of their hardships were due to their faith in Christ. It is easy for money and our possessions to get a hold on us, especially with materialism and greed being so prevalent today. **Are you free from the love of money and possessions?** When I started my business many years ago, I had to face the hold money had on me. I panicked when I didn't have enough of a cushion in my bank account or a few dollars in my pocket. I had to face the fact that I derived a lot of security from money rather than God.

It also takes work to be content with what you have. Once again, I am guilty of seeing what others have and wanting it. I am working at being content with what I have instead of pining away for what I don't have. It isn't always easy. **Are you struggling with the same problem?**

In the context of this issue of money and possessions, the writer quoted a promise seen two other times in the Bible. The Lord promised Joshua (see Joshua 1:5) and Solomon (see 1 Chronicles 28:20) that He would never leave them, and He makes the same promise to us in this verse. If you don't have money or possessions, you have something far greater—God Himself.

How long is "never"? It is a long time! The Lord has promised He will always be with us, never forsaking us.

That is powerful. In these last few decades since I started my ministry, I may not always have had money, but I have found something much better—I have found God. God is faithful, but we are sometimes reminded of that only in hard times.

Brother or sister, do you know God will never leave you? Can you comprehend the wonderful truth of that good news? Money will come and go, possessions will wear out, success may visit and depart. Through it all, however, Jesus has said He will never, ever forsake you. And if Jesus says never, that means never. End of discussion. Amen.

13:6 This verse could have been the motto and the summary for Jesus and His earthly ministry. He completely and totally entrusted Himself to God. On many occasions, He made men angry and they regularly threatened Him, eventually killing Him. Prior to that happening, Jesus had warned His followers:

> "Do not be afraid of those who kill the body but cannot kill the soul. Rather, be afraid of the One who can destroy both soul and body in hell. Are not two sparrows sold for a penny? Yet not one of them will fall to the ground apart from the will of your Father. And even the very hairs of your head are all numbered. So don't be afraid; you are worth more than many sparrows" (Matthew 10:28-31).

What can man do to you? He can reject, criticize, impoverish, torture, and even take your life. That is about it. And in the midst of it all, God can help, save, and preserve you. Daniel's friends knew all this when the king threatened them and then threw them into a red-hot furnace when they refused to bow down to him:

> Furious with rage, King Nebuchadnezzar summoned Shadrach, Meshach and Abednego.

So these men were brought before the king, and Nebuchadnezzar said to them, "Is it true, Shadrach, Meshach and Abednego, that you do not serve my gods or worship the image of gold I have set up? Now when you hear the sound of the horn, flute, zither, lyre, harp, pipes and all kinds of music, if you are ready to fall down and worship the image I made, very good. But if you do not worship it, you will be thrown immediately into a blazing furnace. Then what god will be able to rescue you from my hand?"

Shadrach, Meshach and Abednego replied to the king, "O Nebuchadnezzar, we do not need to defend ourselves before you in this matter. If we are thrown into the blazing furnace, the God we serve is able to save us from it, and he will rescue us from your hand, O king. But even if he does not, we want you to know, O king, that we will not serve your gods or worship the image of gold you have set up." (Daniel 3:13-18).

You have to admire the attitude they had. They knew God could deliver them, but they knew He may not. That fact did not shake their faith or cause them to waver in their commitment. **Does that same knowledge give you the same resolve as they had, that God can but may not deliver you from trouble?**

13:7-8 It seems the writer was not referring to a reader's current spiritual leaders, but those who had given their lives to follow Jesus before the letter was written. Those would have been James the brother of John, Stephen the first martyr. and unnamed others who had exhibited the behavior to which the writer was referring: They did not fear what man could do to them and paid for it with their lives. Remember, the writer's target audience was Christian Jews who were wavering in their faith. James and Stephen would definitely have made an impression on those Jewish believers and would fit into the overall context here. **Who are your spiritual heroes of the past who still speak to you?** Honor their memory by doing what they did.

The writer pointed out that Jesus is the same, the results of faith in Him are the same, and the benefits to His followers who obey Him are the same yesterday, today, and forever. **Isn't it good to know we follow Jesus who never has a bad day, a bad mood, or a "shadow of turning"?** He is consistent and now the challenge is for you to be consistent in following Him, just as those of old were.

> [9] Do not be carried away by all kinds of strange teachings. It is good for our hearts to be strengthened by grace, not by ceremonial foods, which are of no value to those who eat them. [10] We have an altar from which those who minister at the tabernacle have no right to eat. [11] The high priest carries the blood of animals into the Most Holy Place as a sin offering, but the bodies are burned outside the camp. [12] And so Jesus also suffered outside the city gate to make the people holy through his own blood. [13] Let us, then, go to him outside the camp, bearing the disgrace he bore.

13:9 The writer knew there were all kinds of strange doctrines in circulation, and we know that is still true today. He commanded his readers not to be carried away by those strange doctrines, so it must have been within their power not to succumb to them. **How can you follow the same advice and avoid them?** A commitment to God's word is the most important defense. I have found the more I study God's word, the less I can say, "This is what the Lord showed me" or "This is what I think this verse means." I am never free to interpret the Word; the Word interprets itself, and my study causes me to be more careful and disciplined where interpretation is concerned.

Of course, in this context the warning was against any doctrine diminishing the role or importance of Jesus. It's all about Jesus and, no matter how worthy any movement or doctrine sounds, it must stand the "Jesus test." **Does the doctrine you are evaluating exalt Jesus and increase your devotion and commitment to Him?** If not, then leave it alone.

The writer went on to caution the reader against putting any faith in ceremonial foods, which of course Jews were doing at that point in time. As we close this commentary, the writer was still focusing on the main topic: convincing wavering Jews who were followers of Jesus not to abandon their faith for something less. You have to admire the writer's focus. He never wavered from his original theme, and Hebrews is not a short letter.

The Levites were permitted to eat the sacrifices of the Old Testament once the blood had been drained. These foods had no power against sin, however; they were simply for the nourishment and provision of God's servants—and also served as a type of shadow of the main sacrifice to come, the Lamb of God. The writer did not want the readers to do anything that did not benefit them spiritually and, of course, the only true spiritual nourishment was and is Jesus. Jesus Himself said this and many of his followers misunderstood:

Jesus said to them, "I tell you the truth, unless

you eat the flesh of the Son of Man and drink his blood, you have no life in you. Whoever eats my flesh and drinks my blood has eternal life, and I will raise him up at the last day. For my flesh is real food and my blood is real drink. Whoever eats my flesh and drinks my blood remains in me, and I in him. Just as the living Father sent me and I live because of the Father, so the one who feeds on me will live because of me. This is the bread that came down from heaven. Your forefathers ate manna and died, but he who feeds on this bread will live forever" (John 6:53-59).

Are you feasting on Jesus, or is some other food taking up room in your spiritual stomach? Any food except Jesus is like junk food or cotton candy; it looks good, but melts in your mouth and has no nutritional value.

13:10 The Levites had an altar to eat from, but we have another altar, a spiritual one, that only those who call upon the name of Jesus can enjoy. **Are you visiting this altar regularly for the spiritual sustenance you need?**

13:11-13 In other studies, I have pointed out how many things in the Old Testament were a type or shadow of Jesus and the good things to come. The offerings for the forgiveness of sin were no exception. Sin offerings were not consumed but were burned, their remains being carried outside the city or camp and disposed of. That was a shadow of Jesus' sacrifice for sin. What Jesus did, He did alone, separated and apart from public understanding, sympathy, or assistance.

It is good to study the Old Testament but all themes, even in the Old Testament, lead to Jesus. We must always follow those roads, following Jesus in His ministry wherever it may lead us. We must bear some of the disgrace He bore because we are His followers. People seem to have more respect for a religious system because it is easier to comprehend. There is no "system" with Jesus, however, except faith and that offends and even confuses many who want to follow God on their own terms. We must be willing to bear this reproach if we are serious about being His followers. The original readers were evaluating whether that reproach was worth what they were encountering, and some were coming to the conclusion it was not. The writer was trying to convince them it was.

Are you convinced the reproach of Jesus is worth the price you are paying? Don't answer too quickly. **Is your denomination, spiritual heritage, pastor, bishop, or doctrine more important to you than anything else? Would you be willing to walk away from any of that if God wanted you to do so? Does your religious system provide you with the solace and comfort only Jesus can and should provide?** These are serious questions. I have had to face that at times I did indeed put my movement and church affiliation ahead of Him. I trust I have repented, never to repeat that error again.

> ¹⁴For here we do not have an enduring city, but we are looking for the city that is to come. ¹⁵Through Jesus, therefore, let us continually offer to God a sacrifice of praise-the fruit of lips that confess his name. ¹⁶And do not forget to do good and to share with others, for with such sacrifices God is pleased.

13:14 Was the writer making a reference to Jerusalem, the capital of Judaism and a

source of great religious pride among believing and unbelieving Jews? Perhaps he was. It seems, however, that the writer was referring to the pilgrim's mentality, which is a part of every believer's makeup. We know we are citizens of heaven and do not have any lasting inheritance among the kingdoms of the earth:

> For he has rescued us from the dominion of darkness and brought us into the kingdom of the Son he loves, in whom we have redemption, the forgiveness of sins (Colossians 1:13-14).

We are looking for a heavenly Jerusalem, not an earthly one. In chapter eleven, the writer had referred to Abraham, saying: "For he was looking forward to the city with foundations, whose architect and builder is God" (Hebrews 11:10). **If that was Abraham's goal, it should be ours as well, don't you think? What are you looking forward to—a comfortable retirement, or God's will for your life?**

13:15 I have stated this truth throughout these Bible commentaries and will repeat it here: The word sacrifice in this verse does not represent doing something you don't want to do. A biblical concept of sacrifice is giving something to God that already belongs to Him. I have already given God my lips, along with my hands, legs, mind, and heart. To now raise them to praise Him, talk about Him, or serve Him is not a sacrifice. It is an honor and privilege. If you don't want to do any of those things and then do them, it isn't a sacrifice. That shows a hard heart toward God that must be changed through repentance and grace.

13:16 I like the connection here between worship and praise, and practical help you give to other people. You should focus on God in your worship and then focus on man in your service. Paul wrote,

Do not be deceived: God cannot be mocked. A man reaps what he sows. The one who sows to please his sinful nature, from that nature will reap destruction; the one who sows to please the Spirit, from the Spirit will reap eternal life. Let us not become weary in doing good, for at the proper time we will reap a harvest if we do not give up. Therefore, as we have opportunity, let us do good to all people, especially to those who belong to the family of believers (Galatians 6:7-10).

A sacrifice here isn't giving something reluctantly but rather acknowledging that what you are giving to help someone else belongs to God and He is giving it to the person in need through you.

> [17] Obey your leaders and submit to their authority. They keep watch over you as men who must give an account. Obey them so that their work will be a joy, not a burden, for that would be of no advantage to you. [18] Pray for us. We are sure that we have a clear conscience and desire to live honorably in every way. [19] I particularly urge you to pray so that I may be restored to you soon.

13:17 Once the writer urged the readers to follow the lead of those who had gone before them, he then instructed them to obey their current leaders. The work of spiritual oversight is difficult and demanding. The shepherd is required to give an account of those who are under his or her spiritual authority.

When I was a pastor, I can remember some who were

a joy to give care to, and then there were others who were, quite frankly, spiritually obnoxious or demanding. There were some I looked forward to meeting with, and then there were others who required me to take a deep breath and meet with them because Jesus wanted me to do so. I am not sure how spiritual leaders will give an account for their sheep. The principle here is for those who are under authority to have godlike attitudes that will make it easier for spiritual leaders to lead them spiritually.

This also assumes the leaders knew their sheep, something that is much more difficult today in the era of mega churches and "church hopping"—people who move freely from church to church with no point of accountability. **Are you known by a spiritual leader who can give an account of your walk? Do you have access to spiritual help through this leader?**

13:18 The writer requested that the readers pray for his ministry team and for him. **Does this mean the readers knew who wrote this letter? It would seem they did, otherwise how would they know for whom they were praying?** The writer gave a quick account of his own leadership team: They had a clear conscience and lived honorably. That would seem to mean they dealt with any situation that had bothered their conscience or could be cause for accusation. **If you are a leader, can you make the same statement?** I have always tried to use Peter's instructions as a guideline for my own spiritual leadership:

> Be shepherds of God's flock that is under your care, serving as overseers-not because you must, but because you are willing, as God wants you to be; not greedy for money, but eager to serve; not lording it over those entrusted to you, but being examples to the flock. And when the Chief

Shepherd appears, you will receive the crown of glory that will never fade away (1 Peter 5:2-4).

We see that we should pray for our leaders and give them cause for joyful oversight. In turn, leaders should lead the flock not as Gentiles lead, but as Jesus led. **Do you pray for your spiritual leaders? What do you pray? How else can you support them in the work God has given them to do? If you are a leader, are you leading like Jesus?**

13:19 The readers did know who was writing to them and this person had been in their midst. I wonder if the beginning of the letter that contained the writer's name has somehow been lost over time. My own theory is that the writer could not reveal his name since some readers would have been offended or would have rejected the content of the letter because of who wrote it.

That is why I think the apostle Paul wrote this letter or at least collaborated on its content. He was not popular with many Jewish believers, but Paul had a burden to see "his people" come to know Christ. All that, however, is my opinion and theory. If the Holy Spirit wanted us to know who wrote this letter, we would know. We don't, however, so it is only a matter of educated speculation that doesn't really matter much. The important thing is to heed the message in the letter regardless of who wrote it.

> [20]May the God of peace, who through the blood of the eternal covenant brought back from the dead our Lord Jesus, that great Shepherd of the sheep, [21]equip you with everything good for doing his will, and may he work in us what is pleasing to him, through Jesus Christ, to whom be glory for ever and ever. Amen.

13:20-21

What a great prayer these verses contain. If you don't know what to pray, then find the Holy Spirit-inspired prayers of the Bible and pray them. Don't feel pressure to make prayers up; use the ones Scripture provides.

Jesus is the great Shepherd of the sheep. Any pastor is simply an under-shepherd, caring for the flock as Jesus directs. As a pastor, I always took the Lord's words in Ezekiel to heart and I include them here for any pastor or future pastor to consider:

> The word of the Lord came to me. "Son of man, prophesy against the shepherds of Israel; prophesy and say to them: 'This is what the Sovereign Lord says: Woe to the shepherds of Israel who only take care of themselves! Should not shepherds take care of the flock? You eat the curds, clothe yourselves with the wool and slaughter the choice animals, but you do not take care of the flock. You have not strengthened the weak or healed the sick or bound up the injured. You have not brought back the strays or searched for the lost. You have ruled them harshly and brutally. So they were scattered because there was no shepherd, and when they were scattered they became food for all the wild animals. My sheep wandered over all the mountains and on every high hill. They were scattered over the whole earth, and no one searched or looked for them.
>
> "'Therefore, you shepherds, hear the word of the Lord: As surely as I live, declares the Sovereign Lord, because my flock lacks a shepherd and so has been plundered and has become food for all the wild animals, and because my shepherds did not search for my flock but cared for themselves

rather than for my flock, therefore, O shepherds, hear the word of the Lord: This is what the Sovereign Lord says: I am against the shepherds and will hold them accountable for my flock. I will remove them from tending the flock so that the shepherds can no longer feed themselves. I will rescue my flock from their mouths, and it will no longer be food for them.

"'For this is what the Sovereign Lord says: I myself will search for my sheep and look after them. As a shepherd looks after his scattered flock when he is with them, so will I look after my sheep. I will rescue them from all the places where they were scattered on a day of clouds and darkness. I will bring them out from the nations and gather them from the countries, and I will bring them into their own land. I will pasture them on the mountains of Israel, in the ravines and in all the settlements in the land. I will tend them in a good pasture, and the mountain heights of Israel will be their grazing land. There they will lie down in good grazing land, and there they will feed in a rich pasture on the mountains of Israel. I myself will tend my sheep and have them lie down, declares the Sovereign Lord. I will search for the lost and bring back the strays. I will bind up the injured and strengthen the weak, but the sleek and the strong I will destroy. I will shepherd the flock with justice" (Ezekiel 34:1-16).

As you read this long passage, can you identify the main objectives God wants any shepherd to have? Do you follow these objectives? Does your own spiritual leadership exhibit these characteristics?

²²Brothers, I urge you to bear with my word of exhortation, for I have written you only a short letter. ²³I want you to know that our brother Timothy has been released. If he arrives soon, I will come with him to see you. ²⁴Greet all your leaders and all God's people. Those from Italy send you their greetings. ²⁵Grace be with you all.

13:22 **I don't consider this a short letter, do you?** It is one of the longer letters included in the New Testament. This letter was intended to exhort those wavering in the faith to stabilize and return to the better covenant offered in Christ. **Do you think the writer achieved his purpose for which he wrote the letter?** He made his case, but we will never know how the readers responded.

I am more and more impressed with writing as a means to communicate, maintain, direct, and even rebuke in the ministry of a pastor. I have always been hesitant to write letters and even urged people whom I counseled not to write letters but rather to go to the person or persons involved. I am seeing the value of leaving a written record and in giving people something to read and re-read. Obviously, the Holy Spirit thought letters were a good idea, for much of the New Testament is made up of letters. **So, are you ready to do more writing?** Modern technology makes this easier than ever before.

13:23 This one verse sounds like Paul wrote this because he spoke about Timothy in such familiar terms—but we cannot say for sure. We can say with certainty, however, that Timothy was a faithful brother who served Paul and the Lord with distinction. Here is what Paul wrote about him in his letter to the Philippians:

> I hope in the Lord Jesus to send Timothy to you soon, that I also may be cheered when I receive news about you. I have no one else like him, who takes a genuine interest in your welfare. For everyone looks out for his own interests, not those of Jesus Christ. But you know that Timothy has proved himself, because as a son with his father he has served with me in the work of the gospel. I hope, therefore, to send him as soon as I see how things go with me. And I am confident in the Lord that I myself will come soon (Philippians 2:19-24).

I have made it my goal to be like Timothy: faithful in the service of others. This can be difficult to achieve, however, for it requires dying to self and living for the benefit of others. If Paul only saw one like Timothy in his ministry, then a man like Timothy must be a rare thing. Even if you can't attain to Timothy's faithfulness, however, you can still *try* to do so. **The church of Jesus will be the better for your efforts, don't you agree?**

13:24-25 The last words of the letter included the word *grace*. It is obvious that the writer, even though he wrote some harsh things, wanted the grace of God to abound in the lives of the readers. **Is that your goal when you deal with God's people? Is grace your goal?** If not, it should be.

And I hope grace is what you have received from this study of Hebrews. As we complete another study, I urge you to continue your studies of God's word. Devote time to this study and go to school if you can. Read and continue to learn and grow in the knowledge of God. I pray the Lord will use this study and all the studies I have produced to bring grace and peace to you and yours. God bless you. Amen.

About the Author

John Stanko was born in Pittsburgh, Pennsylvania. After graduating from St. Basil's Prep School in Stamford, Connecticut, he attended Duquesne University where he received his bachelor's and master's degrees in economics in 1972 and 1974 respectively.

Since then, John has served as an administrator, teacher, consultant, author, and pastor in his profession-al career. He holds a second master's degree in pastoral ministries, and earned his doctorate in pastoral ministries from Liberty Theological Seminary in Houston, Texas in 1995. He completed a second doctor of ministry degree at Reformed Presbyterian Theological Seminary in Pittsburgh.

John has taught extensively on the topics of time management, life purpose and organization, and has conducted leadership and purpose training sessions throughout the United States and in 32 countries. He is also certified to administer the DISC and other related personality assessments as well as the Natural Church Development profile for churches. In 2006, he earned the privilege to facilitate for The Pacific Institute of Seattle, a leadership and personal development program, and for The Leadership Circle, a provider of cultural and executive 360-degree profiles. He has authored fifteen books and written for many publications around the world.

John founded a personal and leadership development company, called PurposeQuest, in 2001 and today travels the world to speak, consult and inspire leaders and people everywhere. From 2001-2008, he spent six months a year in Africa and still enjoys visiting and working on that continent, while teaching for Geneva College's Masters of Organizational Leadership and the Center for

Urban Biblical Ministry in his hometown of Pittsburgh, Pennsylvania. John has been married for 44 years to Kathryn Scimone Stanko, and they have two adult children and two grandchildren. In 2009, John was appointed the administrative pastor for discipleship at Allegheny Center Alliance Church on the North Side of Pittsburgh where he served for five years. Most recently, John founded Urban Press, a publishing service designed to tell stories of the city, from the city, and to the city.

Keep in Touch with John W. Stanko

www.purposequest.com
www.johnstanko.us
www.stankobiblestudy.com
www.stankomondaymemo.com
or via email at johnstanko@gmail.com

John also does extensive relief and community development work in Kenya. You can see some of his projects at www.purposequest.com/contributions

PurposeQuest International
PO Box 8882
Pittsburgh, PA 15221-0882

Additional Titles by John W. Stanko

A Daily Dose of Proverbs
A Daily Taste of Proverbs
Changing the Way We Do Church
I Wrote This Book on Purpose
Life Is A Gold Mine: Can You Dig It?
Strictly Business
The Faith Files, Volume 1
The Faith Files, Volume 2
The Faith Files, Volume 3
The Leadership Walk
The Price of Leadership
Unlocking the Power of Your Creativity
Unlocking the Power of Your Productivity
Unlocking the Power of Your Purpose
Unlocking the Power of You
What Would Jesus Ask You Today?
Your Life Matters

Live the Word Commentary: Matthew
Live the Word Commentary: Mark
Live the Word Commentary: Luke
Live the Word Commentary: John
Live the Word Commentary: Acts
Live the Word Commentary: Romans
Live the Word Commentary: 1 & 2 Corinthians
Live the Word Commentary: Galatians, Ephesians, Philippians, Colossians, Philemon
Live the Word Commentary: Revelation

www.ingramcontent.com/pod-product-compliance
Lightning Source LLC
LaVergne TN
LVHW051117080426
835510LV00018B/2087